FISH & SEAFOOD

FISH & SEAFOOD

175 DELICIOUS CLASSIC AND CONTEMPORARY FISH RECIPES
SHOWN IN 220 STUNNING PHOTOGRAPHS

Anne Hildyard

LORENZ BOOKS

This edition is published by Lorenz Books,
an imprint of Anness Publishing Ltd, Blaby Road,
Wigston, Leicestershire LE18 4SE; info@anness.com

www.lorenzbooks.com; www.annesspublishing.com

If you like the images in this book and would like to investigate using them
for publishing, promotions or advertising, please visit our website
www.practicalpictures.com for more information.

Publisher: Joanna Lorenz
Executive Editor: Joanne Rippin
Designer: Adelle Morris
Production controller: Wendy Lawson

© Anness Publishing Ltd 2013

NOTES

Bracketed terms are intended for American readers.

For all recipes, quantities are given in both metric and imperial measures
and, where appropriate, in standard cups and spoons. Follow one set of
measures, but not a mixture, because they are not interchangeable.

Standard spoon and cup measures are level. 1 tsp = 5ml, 1 tbsp = 15ml,
1 cup = 250ml/8fl oz.
Australian standard tablespoons are 20ml. Australian readers should use
3 tsp in place of 1 tbsp for measuring small quantities.
American pints are 16fl oz/2 cups. American readers should use
20fl oz/2.5 cups in place of 1 pint when measuring liquids.

Electric oven temperatures in this book are for conventional ovens.
When using a fan oven, the temperature will probably need to be reduced
by about 10–20°C/20–40°F. Since ovens vary, you should check with your
manufacturer's instruction book for guidance.

The nutritional analysis given for each recipe is calculated per portion
(i.e. serving or item), unless otherwise stated. If the recipe gives a range,
such as Serves 4–6, then the nutritional analysis will be for the smaller
portion size, i.e. 6 servings. The analysis does not include optional
ingredients, such as salt added to taste.

Medium (US large) eggs are used unless otherwise stated.

Contents

Introduction

Fish is one of healthiest proteins available; it is low in fat and in cholesterol, and is high in both minerals and vitamins. Eating just one portion of oily fish each week is said to be enough to contribute to the well-being of your heart by lowering cholesterol levels and helping to clear blocked arteries. Not only does it have great health benefits, seafood is also one of the most delicious ingredients available, and offers an amazing range of different types.

The infinite variety of fish and shellfish in markets and stores is matched by the many ways of cooking and preparing this most delightful of foods. The busy pace of life can mean that people do not believe they have time to cook or prepare fish, but most fishmongers will help by filleting and cleaning the fish, and prepared fillets are available at supermarkets. In fact, fish is quicker and easier to cook than foods such as meat, which require some knowledge and judgement to cook correctly.

Fish and shellfish can be used for every type of savoury dish, from appetizers and main courses to salads and soups. Fish lends itself to robust spicy flavours as well as to delicate creamy sauces and tangy dressings. Each type of fish has a unique taste that can be enhanced with perfectly balanced sauces and seasonings.

BELOW: *Cooking marinated brochettes of white fish using a hot grill (griddle) is one of the best ways to flash-cook fish.*

ABOVE: *Red mullet has delicate flesh and a beautiful red skin.*

ABOVE: *Steaks of tender tuna are perfect for a quick supper.*

ABOVE: *Large prawns (jumbo shrimp) carry hot and spicy flavours really well.*

USING THIS BOOK

This collection of recipes provides a fantastic resource when cooking any type of fish or shellfish. All the classic dishes are here: Bouillabaisse, Ceviche, Tuna Salad Niçoise, Halibut Steaks with Lemon Butter and Classic Fish Pie. There is also a wide selection of unusual and tempting dishes from all over the world, from East to West, and covering many of the renowned fish-loving cuisines, from Norway to Vietnam.

The recipes are divided into six chapters: Soups and Appetizers; Salads; Pasta and Rice; Poached, Grilled and Steamed; Fried and Baked; Pies, Gratins and Bakes; and Casseroles and Curries, so it is easy to find the perfect dish for any occasion.

Whether you are looking for a midweek family dish, a tasty lunch or an elegant dinner party menu, you will find a recipe that your family or guests will enjoy. Enjoy the best of fish and shellfish cooking with Fried Squid with Salt and Pepper from Saigon; Chilli Crab Cakes and Crispy Egg Noodle Pancake with Prawns from China; and Scallops and Squid, or Paella Valenciana from Spain. Scandinavia has a rich tradition of cooking fish and seafood, and several of its classic dishes are included, such as Chopped Herring Salad; Salt Cod with Mustard Sauce and Fried Eel with Potatoes in Cream Sauce.

The ingredients used in the recipes in this book include a huge variety of fish and seafood, from anchovies to whelks. The 150 tempting recipes, with clearly explained steps, are illustrated with attractive photographs to show the finished dish, with full nutritional notes for each recipe.

With so many dishes to choose from, and a wide range of fish and shellfish available, there is sure to be a dish here to tempt every palate, for every occasion and season.

Soups and Appetizers

Fish soups are a wonderful way to make the most of your local fishmonger's catch of the day, as the choice of ingredients is so flexible. Rich and sustaining, fish soups often make a meal on their own. Appetizers, on the other hand, use specific types of fish in creamy mousses, marinated fishes, and tempting fried morsels, all of which make the perfect start to a meal.

Mediterranean seafood soup

For this delicious soup, you need firm fish that will not fall apart while cooking. If you can't obtain monkfish or red mullet, substitute cod, haddock or hake. The rouille enriches the finished dish, and if you have time to make your own mayonnaise it will be even more special.

SERVES 4

450g/1lb fresh clams, scrubbed, discarding any
    that do not shut when tapped

120ml/4fl oz/½ cup white wine

15ml/1 tbsp olive oil

4 garlic cloves, crushed

5ml/1 tsp fennel seeds

a pinch of dried chilli flakes

1 fennel bulb, halved and sliced

1 red pepper, seeded and sliced

8 plum tomatoes, halved

1 onion, cut into thin wedges

225g/8oz waxy potatoes, sliced

1 bay leaf

1 sprig fresh thyme

600ml/1 pint/2½ cups fish stock

1 mini French stick

225g/8oz monkfish fillet, cut into chunks

350g/12oz red mullet or snapper fillet, cut into chunks

45ml/3 tbsp Pernod

salt and ground black pepper

fennel fronds, to garnish

FOR THE ROUILLE

a few saffron threads

150ml/¼ pint/⅔ cup mayonnaise

a dash of Tabasco sauce

1 Place the clams in a pan with the wine. Cover and cook over a high heat for 4 minutes, until opened. Drain, strain, and reserve the liquid. Discard any unopened clams and reserve 8 in their shells. Shell the remaining clams.

2 Heat the oil and add the garlic, fennel seeds and chilli flakes, and cook for about 2 minutes. Add the sliced fennel, pepper, tomatoes, onion and reserved cooking liquid. Cover and simmer for 10 minutes. Add the potatoes, bay leaf and thyme, and the fish stock. Cover and cook for 15–20 minutes.

3 To make the saffron rouille, pound the saffron to a powder, then beat it into the mayonnaise and Tabasco. Add the fish and Pernod to the soup and cook for 3–4 minutes. Add all the clams and heat for 30 seconds. Remove the bay leaf and thyme sprig, and season well.

4 Cut the French stick into eight thin slices and toast on both sides. Spoon the rouille on to the toasts. Ladle the soup into bowls, garnish with a frond of fennel and serve with the toasts.

Nutritional information per portion: Energy 728Kcal/3048kJ; Protein 50.2g; Carbohydrate 40g, of which sugars 10.9g; Fat 37.1g, of which saturates 5.4g; Cholesterol 111mg; Calcium 238mg; Fibre 4.7g; Sodium 1200mg.

Seafood soup

Whenever you prepare a dish with large prawns or fish fillets, save the heads and bones and freeze them until you have enough to make a flavoursome stock, such as the one in this recipe.

SERVES 6

60ml/4 tbsp olive oil

2kg/4½ lb prawn (shrimp) heads and fish bones

1kg/2¼ lb mixed onions, carrots, leek, and garlic, chopped

1 bay leaf

6 black peppercorns

105ml/7 tbsp dry white wine

1 green and 1 red (bell) pepper, seeded and finely diced

1 onion, chopped

2 ripe tomatoes, peeled and diced

1 garlic clove, chopped

15ml/1 tbsp chopped fresh thyme

185g/6½ oz clams, scrubbed, discarding any that do not close when tapped

125g/4¼ oz prepared squid

300g/11oz white fish fillet, cut in chunks

12 prawns (shrimp), peeled

chopped coriander (cilantro), to garnish

1 Heat 30ml/2 tbsp of the olive oil in a pan. Add the prawn heads and cook on a low heat for 5 minutes.

2 Add the vegetables, bay leaf and peppercorns and cook for 5 minutes. Mash the prawn heads with a spoon.

3 Pour in the wine and 2 litres/ 3½ pints/8¾ cups water. Bring to the boil, then lower the heat and simmer gently for 1 hour.

4 Add the fish bones and bring to the boil. Lower the heat and simmer very gently for 20 minutes. Strain the stock into a bowl.

5 Heat the remaining olive oil in a clean pan. Add the peppers, onion and tomatoes, and cook over a low heat, stirring, for 5 minutes, until the vegetables have softened.

6 Add the garlic and thyme to the pan, pour in the stock and bring just to the boil.

7 Add the clams and squid to the stock and cook for 2–3 minutes, until the clams have opened.

8 Add the fish and prawns and cook for 5 minutes more. Sprinkle with coriander and serve.

Nutritional information per portion: Energy 267kcal/1112kJ; Protein 20.1g; Carbohydrate 25.2g, of which sugars 18.7g; Fat 9g, of which saturates 1.3g; Cholesterol 96mg; Calcium 96mg; Fibre 4.8g; Sodium 262mg.

Fish soup with salted cucumber

This fish dish is considered to be the queen of Russian soups. Its lovely, rich flavour is accentuated by the piquant additions of capers, salted cucumbers and olives.

SERVES 4

2 onions, finely chopped

2–3 carrots, peeled and diced

1 parsnip, peeled and diced

200g/7oz salted cucumbers, finely diced

30–45ml/2–3 tbsp rapeseed (canola) oil

15ml/1 tbsp tomato purée (paste)

4–5 black peppercorns

1 litre/1¾ pints/4 cups fish stock

8 green olives and 8 black olives

30ml/2 tbsp capers plus 5ml/1 tsp brine
    from the jar

400–500g/14oz–1¼lb salmon, halibut
    and turbot fillets, skinned and cubed

4 thin lemon slices and chopped fresh dill,
    to garnish

60ml/4 tbsp crème fraîche, to serve

1 Heat the oil in a large pan, add the onions and fry over a medium heat for 2–3 minutes, until softened.

2 Add the carrots and parsnip and fry, stirring, for 5 minutes.

3 Add the diced cucumbers, tomato purée and peppercorns to the pan and fry for 2–3 minutes more. Add half of the stock, cover and bring to the boil. Reduce the heat and simmer for 10 minutes.

4 Add the remaining stock, olives, capers, and brine from the jar to the pan. Return to the boil and add the fish cubes. Reduce the heat and simmer for 5 minutes, until the fish is just tender, being careful not to overcook the fish.

5 Spoon the soup into warm bowls, add a slice of lemon, and garnish with some chopped dill. Offer a bowl of crème fraîche for guests to add a spoonful if they wish.

Nutritional information per portion: Energy 389kcal/1613kJ; Protein 24.5g; Carbohydrate 9.1g, of which sugars 7.2g; Fat 28.5g, of which saturates 7.7g; Cholesterol 73mg; Calcium 74mg; Fibre 3.1g; Sodium 361mg.

Peruvian-style fish soup

A small town in Peru, called Chilca, has contributed this style of fish soup – enriched with lime and chilli – to the national cuisine. Sometimes it is made with just the heads of the fish (an economical version often cooked by students), at other times a whole fish or shellfish is used, but for the soup to be a genuine chilcano it is important to make this with only one type of fish.

SERVES 6

2 litres/3½ pints/8 cups water

2 medium white fish, such as sea bass, about
   1kg/2¼lb total weight, cleaned and gutted

2 garlic cloves, very finely chopped

1 small red onion, finely chopped

1 spring onion (scallion), finely chopped

1 red chilli, seeded and finely chopped

juice of ½ lime, plus wedges for serving

30ml/2 tbsp finely chopped parsley

salt and ground black pepper

1 Bring the water to the boil in a large pan with the garlic, red onion, and half the spring onion, chilli and parsley. When it bubbles, lay the whole fish in the pan. Season. Return to the boil, reduce the heat, cover and simmer for 10 minutes.

2 Lift out the fish and leave the soup simmering, uncovered, for a further 15–20 minutes to reduce and concentrate the flavour.

3 Meanwhile, remove the heads and tails from the fish, take off the fillets and divide into individual portions. Keep warm.

4 Strain the soup and adjust the seasoning. Divide the pieces of fish among hot bowls, pour over the soup, garnish with the reserved spring onion, chilli, lime juice and parsley, and serve with wedges of lime for squeezing over.

COOK'S TIP

Although only one type of fish is used, this can vary from sea bass to any firm white fish. The soup can also be made with prawns (shrimps), crabs, or mussels, depending on the ingredients to hand.

Nutritional information per portion: Energy 145kcal/610kJ; Protein 31g; Carbohydrate 1.1g, of which sugars 0.8g; Fat 1.9g, of which saturates 0.7g; Cholesterol 87mg; Calcium 63mg; Fibre 0.6g; Sodium 164mg.

Filipino fish soup with spiked suka

Chunky and satisfying, Filipino fish soups come in many varieties, depending on the region and local fish, but most are flavoured with sour tamarind and served with coconut vinegar, or suka.

SERVES 4–6

2 litres/3½ pints/8 cups fish stock

250ml/8fl oz/1 cup white wine

15–30ml/1–2 tbsp tamarind paste

30–45ml/2–3 tbsp patis (Filipino fish sauce)

30ml/2 tbsp palm sugar (jaggery)

50g/2oz fresh root ginger, grated

2–3 fresh red or green chillies, seeded and finely sliced

2 tomatoes, skinned, seeded and cut into wedges

350g/12oz fresh fish, such as trout, sea bass, swordfish or cod, cut into bitesize chunks

12–16 fresh prawns (shrimp), in their shells

a bunch of fresh basil leaves, torn

a bunch of fresh flat leaf parsley, roughly chopped

salt and ground black pepper

FOR THE SPIKED SUKA

60–90ml/4–6 tbsp suka (Filipino coconut vinegar)

1–2 garlic cloves, finely chopped

1–2 limes, cut into wedges

2 fresh red or green chillies, seeded and quartered lengthways

1 In a wok or large pan, bring the stock and wine to the boil. Stir in the tamarind paste, patis, sugar, ginger and chillies. Reduce the heat and simmer for 15–20 minutes. Add the tomatoes to the broth and season with salt and pepper.

2 Add the chunks of fish and the prawns and simmer for a further 5 minutes, until the fish is cooked and flakes easily. Meanwhile, in a bowl, quickly mix together the suka and garlic for serving and put aside.

3 Stir half the basil and half the parsley into the broth and ladle into bowls. Garnish with the remaining basil and parsley and serve with the spiked suka to splash on top, the lime wedges to squeeze into the soup, and the chillies to chew on for those who like extra heat.

Nutritional information per portion: Energy 137kcal/576kJ; Protein 17.7g; Carbohydrate 8.1g, of which sugars 8g; Fat 1g, of which saturates 0.1g; Cholesterol 92mg; Calcium 76mg; Fibre 1.3g; Sodium 644mg.

Prawn wonton soup

The light stock for this wonton soup derives its richness from dried fish like sprats or anchovies. While Chinese stores sell instant wonton soup stock, it is easy to make your own.

SERVES 4

60g/2oz dried sprats or anchovies
750ml/1¼ pints/3 cups water
15ml/1 tbsp light soy sauce
chopped spring onions (scallions),
    to garnish

FOR THE WONTONS

300g/11oz raw prawns (shrimp), peeled
    and deveined and very finely chopped
    or briefly pulsed in a food processor
15ml/1 tbsp light soy sauce
15ml/1 tbsp sesame oil
2.5ml/½ tsp ground black pepper
15ml/1 tbsp cornflour (cornstarch)
16 wonton wrappers

1 Scrape the chopped prawns into a bowl and add the soy sauce, sesame oil, pepper and cornflour. Mix well.

2 Place about 5ml/1 tsp of the mixture in the centre of a wonton wrapper, bring the edges together so that they meet at the top, and pinch to seal. Fill the rest of the wontons in the same way.

3 Bring a small pan of water to the boil. Add the wontons and cook them for 5 minutes. Drain.

4 Transfer the wontons to a bowl and toss with a little oil to prevent them from sticking together. Put the dried sprats or anchovies in a large pan with the water.

5 Add the soy sauce to the pan and bring to the boil. Cook for 5 minutes. Add more soy sauce if needed.

6 Strain the soup, return to the pan and heat. Place four wontons in each soup bowl, add the soup, garnish with spring onions, and serve.

Nutritional information per portion: Energy 178kcal/748kJ; Protein 19g; Carbohydrate 15.2g, of which sugars 0.8g; Fat 4.9g, of which saturates 0.8g; Cholesterol 156mg; Calcium 132mg; Fibre 0.6g; Sodium 1267mg.

Hot and sour fish soup

This unusual, vibrantly coloured and tangy soup can be found throughout South-east Asia. Chillies provide the heat and tamarind produces the tartness.

SERVES 4

1 catfish, sea bass or red snapper, about
    1kg/2¼lb, filleted
25g/1oz dried squid, soaked in water for
    30 minutes
15ml/1 tbsp vegetable oil
2 spring onions (scallions), sliced
2 shallots, sliced
4cm/1½ in fresh root ginger, peeled and chopped
2–3 lemon grass stalks, cut into strips
    and crushed
30ml/2 tbsp tamarind paste
2–3 Thai chillies, seeded and sliced
15ml/1 tbsp sugar
30–45ml/2–3 tbsp Thai fish sauce

225g/8oz fresh pineapple, peeled and diced
3 tomatoes, skinned, seeded and
    roughly chopped
50g/2oz canned sliced bamboo shoots, drained
1 small bunch of fresh coriander (cilantro),
    stalks removed, leaves finely chopped
salt and ground black pepper
115g/4oz/½cup beansprouts and a bunch of
    dill, fronds roughly chopped, to garnish
1 lime, cut into wedges, to serve

FOR THE MARINADE
30ml/2 tbsp fish sauce
2 garlic cloves, finely chopped

1 Cut the fish into bitesize pieces. Reserve the head, tail and bones for the stock. In a bowl, mix the marinade ingredients and add the fish. Set aside. Drain and rinse the squid.

2 Heat the oil in a deep pan and stir in the spring onions, shallots, ginger, lemon grass and squid. Add the reserved fish head, tail and bones, and sauté them gently for 2 minutes. Pour in 1.2 litres/2 pints/5 cups water and bring to the boil. Reduce the heat and simmer for 30 minutes.

3 Strain the stock into another pan and bring to the boil. Add the tamarind paste, chillies, sugar and fish sauce and simmer for 2–3 minutes. Add the pineapple, tomatoes and bamboo shoots and simmer for 2–3 minutes. Stir in the fish pieces and the coriander, and cook until the fish turns opaque.

4 Season and ladle the soup into hot bowls. Garnish with beansprouts and dill, and serve with the lime wedges.

Nutritional information per portion: Energy 335Kcal/1415kJ; Protein 44g; Carbohydrate 24g, of which sugars 19g; Fat 7g, of which saturates 1g; Cholesterol 108mg; Calcium 138mg; Fibre 2.3g; Sodium 1.2mg.

Chinese fish ball soup

This light soup can be found in Chinese street stalls, where the food is cooked on the spot. Often eaten as a snack or light lunch, it is garnished with spring onions and fresh chillies.

SERVES 4–6

FOR THE FISH BALLS
450g/1lb fresh fish fillets (such as haddock, cod, whiting or bream), boned and flaked
15–30ml/1–2 tbsp rice flour
salt and ground black pepper

FOR THE SOUP
1.5 litres/2½ pints/6¼ cups fish stock
15–30ml/1–2 tbsp light soy sauce
4–6 mustard green leaves, shredded
90g/3½ oz mung bean thread noodles, soaked in hot water until soft

FOR THE GARNISH
2 spring onions (scallions), trimmed and finely sliced
1 red chilli, seeded and sliced
fresh coriander (cilantro) leaves, finely chopped

1 To make the fish balls, grind the flaked fish fillets to a paste, using a mortar and pestle or a food processor. Season with salt and pepper and stir in 60ml/4 tbsp water. Add enough rice flour to form a paste. Roll into small balls.

2 Bring the stock to the boil and season to taste with soy sauce.

3 Drop in the fish balls and simmer for 5 minutes. Add the shredded greens and cook for 1 minute.

4 Divide the noodles among four to six bowls. Using a slotted spoon, add the fish balls and greens to the noodles, then ladle over the hot stock. Garnish with the spring onions and chilli and sprinkle the chopped coriander over the top.

Nutritional information per portion: Energy 127Kcal/533kJ; Protein 14.9g; Carbohydrate 14.8g, of which sugars 0.5g; Fat 0.6g, of which saturates 0.1g; Cholesterol 35mg; Calcium 17mg; Fibre 0.2g; Sodium 408mg.

Smoked haddock chowder with sweet Thai basil

Based on a traditional Scottish recipe, this soup has American-style sweetness from the sweet potatoes and butternut squash, and is flavoured with a hint of Thai basil.

SERVES 4

400g/14oz sweet potatoes (pink-fleshed variety), cubed and cooked in salted water for 15 minutes

225g/8oz peeled butternut squash, cut into 1cm/½ in slices and cooked in salted water for 15 minutes

50g/2oz/¼ cup butter

1 onion, chopped

450g/1lb smoked haddock fillets, skinned

300ml/½ pint/1¼ cups water

600ml/1 pint/2½ cups milk

a small handful of Thai basil leaves

60ml/4 tbsp double (heavy) cream

salt and ground black pepper

1 Melt half the butter in a large, heavy pan. Add the onion and cook for 4–5 minutes, until softened but not browned. Add the haddock fillets and water.

2 Bring to the boil, reduce the heat and simmer for 10 minutes, until the fish is cooked. Use a slotted spoon to lift the fish out of the pan and leave to cool. Set the cooking liquid aside.

3 When cool enough to handle, break the flesh into large flakes, discarding the skin and bones.

4 Mash the sweet potatoes until smooth and beat in the remaining butter with seasoning to taste.

5 Strain the reserved fish cooking liquid and return it to the rinsed-out pan, then whisk in the sweet potato. Stir in the milk and bring to the boil. Simmer for about 2–3 minutes.

6 Stir in the butternut squash, fish, Thai basil leaves and cream. Season the soup to taste and heat through without bringing to the boil. Ladle the soup into six warmed soup bowls and serve.

Nutritional information per portion: Energy 258kcal/1196kJ; Protein 19.1g; Carbohydrate 20.7g, of which sugars 9.9g; Fat 14.7g, of which saturates 8.9g; Cholesterol 64mg; Calcium 166mg; Fibre 2.1g; Sodium 173mg.

Mullet and fennel soup

This soup is enriched with aioli, the deliciously rich Mediterranean garlic mayonnaise. Crisp olive and tomato toasts make a lovely crunchy accompaniment.

SERVES 4

25ml/1½ tbsp olive oil
1 onion, chopped
3 garlic cloves, chopped
2 fennel bulbs, thinly sliced
4 tomatoes, chopped
1 bay leaf
sprig of fresh thyme
1.2 litres/2 pints/5 cups fish stock
675g/1½ lb red mullet or snapper, scaled and filleted and cut into two or three pieces
salt and ground black pepper

FOR THE TOASTS

8 slices French stick, toasted
1 garlic clove
30ml/2 tbsp tomato purée (paste)
12 black olives, stoned (pitted) and quartered
fresh fennel fronds, to garnish

FOR THE AIOLI

2 egg yolks
1–2 garlic cloves, crushed
10ml/2 tsp lemon juice
300ml/½ pint/1¼ cups virgin olive oil

1 Heat the olive oil in a large pan. Add the onion and garlic and cook for 5 minutes, until soft. Add the fennel and cook for 2–3 minutes. Stir in the tomatoes, bay leaf, thyme and stock. Boil, reduce the heat, cover and simmer for 30 minutes.

2 To make the aioli, whisk the egg yolks, garlic, lemon juice and seasoning in a large bowl. Whisk in the oil, drop by drop. As it begins to thicken, add the oil in a slow trickle.

3 Add the pieces of mullet to the soup and cook gently for 5 minutes. Remove the fish and set aside.

4 Strain the cooking liquid, pressing the vegetables well. Whisk a ladleful of soup into the aioli, then whisk in the remaining soup in one go.

5 Return the soup to a clean pan and cook gently, whisking all the time, until the mixture is slightly thickened. Add the fish pieces.

6 Rub the French bread toasts with garlic, spread with tomato purée and top with olives. Serve the soup topped with the toasts and garnished with fennel.

Nutritional information per portion: Energy 492kcal/2079kJ; Protein 41.2g; Carbohydrate 53.6g, of which sugars 10g; Fat 14.1g, of which saturates 1.2g; Cholesterol 0mg; Calcium 256mg; Fibre 6.1g; Sodium 965mg.

Pad Thai red monkfish soup

This light and creamy coconut soup provides a base for a colourful fusion of red-curried monkfish and pad Thai, the classic stir-fried noodle dish of Thailand.

SERVES 4

175g/6oz flat rice noodles
30ml/2 tbsp vegetable oil
2 garlic cloves, chopped
15ml/1 tbsp red curry paste
450g/1lb monkfish tail, cut into pieces
300ml/½ pint/1¼ cups coconut cream
750ml/1¼ pints/3 cups hot chicken stock
45ml/3 tbsp Thai fish sauce
15ml/1 tbsp palm sugar (jaggery)
60ml/4 tbsp roasted peanuts, roughly
    chopped
4 spring onions (scallions), shredded
    lengthways
50g/2oz beansprouts
a large handful of fresh Thai basil leaves
salt and ground black pepper
1 red chilli, seeded and cut lengthways
    into slivers, to garnish

1 Soak the noodles in boiling water for 10 minutes, or according to the packet instructions. Drain.

2 Heat the oil in a wok or large pan over a high heat. Add the garlic and cook for 2 minutes. Stir in the curry paste and cook for 1 minute until fragrant.

3 Add the monkfish and stir-fry over a high heat for 4–5 minutes, until just tender. Pour in the coconut cream and stock.

4 Stir in the fish sauce and sugar, and bring to the boil. Add the drained noodles and cook over a medium heat for 1–2 minutes.

5 Stir in half the peanuts, half the spring onions, half the beansprouts, the basil and season to taste.

6 Ladle the soup into warmed bowls and sprinkle over the remaining peanuts. Garnish with the remaining spring onions, beansprouts and the slivers of red chilli.

Nutritional information per portion: Energy 379kcal/1589kJ; Protein 25.5g; Carbohydrate 41.2g, of which sugars 4.7g; Fat 12g, of which saturates 2g; Cholesterol 18mg; Calcium 49mg; Fibre 0.9g; Sodium 111mg.

Noodle, pak choi and seared salmon ramen

Ramen is a Japanese noodle soup for which a good stock is essential. Here, the lightly spiced broth is enhanced by slices of fresh salmon and crisp vegetables.

SERVES 4

1.5 litres/2½ pints/6¼ cups good
  vegetable stock
2.5cm/1in piece fresh root ginger, finely
  sliced
2 garlic cloves, crushed
6 spring onions (scallions), sliced
45ml/3 tbsp soy sauce
45ml/3 tbsp sake
450g/1lb salmon fillet, skinned and
  boned
5ml/1 tsp groundnut oil
350g/12oz ramen or udon noodles
4 small heads pak choi (bok choy), broken
  into leaves
1 red chilli, seeded and sliced
50g/2oz/¼ cup beansprouts
salt and ground black pepper

1 Pour the stock into a large pan and add the ginger, garlic, and a third of the spring onions. Add the soy sauce and sake. Bring to the boil, then reduce the heat; simmer for 30 minutes.

2 Meanwhile, remove any pin bones from the salmon using tweezers, then cut the salmon on the slant into 12 slices, using a sharp knife.

3 Brush a ridged griddle or frying pan with the oil and heat until very hot. Sear the salmon for 1–2 minutes on each side until tender and marked by the ridges of the pan. Set aside.

4 Cook the ramen or udon noodles in boiling water for 4–5 minutes or according to the packet instructions. Drain and refresh under cold running water. Drain again and set aside.

5 Strain the broth into a clean pan and season, then bring to the boil. Add the pak choi leaves to the pan.

6 Twist the noodles into four nests with a fork and place into bowls. Add three slices of salmon to each bowl. Divide the remaining spring onions, chilli and beansprouts among the bowls, then ladle the broth around the ingredients.

Nutritional information per portion: Energy 572kcal/2406kJ; Protein 34.1g; Carbohydrate 65.2g, of which sugars 3.1g; Fat 21.2g, of which saturates 4.6g; Cholesterol 83mg; Calcium 150mg; Fibre 4g; Sodium 826mg.

Rocket soup with kiln-smoked salmon

Kiln-smoked salmon has actually been cooked during the smoking process, producing a delicious flaky texture, in contrast to traditional cold-smoked salmon, which is preserved first in brine.

SERVES 4

15ml/1 tbsp olive oil
1 small onion, sliced
1 garlic clove, crushed
150ml/¼ pint/²/₃ cup double
    (heavy) cream
350ml/12fl oz/1½ cups vegetable stock
350g/12oz rocket (arugula)
4 fresh basil leaves
salt and ground black pepper
flaked kiln-smoked salmon, to garnish

VARIATION
Cold-smoked salmon can also be used. Simply cut a few slices into medium to thick strips and add to the hot soup.

1 Put the olive oil in a high-sided pan over a medium heat and allow to heat up. Add the sliced onion and sweat for a few minutes, stirring continuously. Add the garlic and continue to sweat until soft and transparent, although you should not allow the onion to colour.

2 Add the cream and stock to the pan, stir in gently and bring slowly to the boil. Allow to simmer gently for about 5 minutes.

3 Add the rocket, reserving a few leaves to garnish, and the basil. Return briefly to the boil and turn off the heat. Add a little cold water and allow to cool for a few minutes.

4 Purée in a blender until smooth, adding salt and pepper to taste. When ready to serve, reheat gently but do not allow to boil. Serve in warmed bowls with a few flakes of salmon, a leaf or two of rocket and a drizzle of virgin olive oil.

Nutritional information per portion: Energy 258kcal/1063kJ; Protein 6.8g; Carbohydrate 3.2g, of which sugars 2.8g; Fat 24.3g, of which saturates 13.1g; Cholesterol 56mg; Calcium 174mg; Fibre 2.1g; Sodium 395mg.

Soup niçoise with seared tuna

The ingredients for the classic salad from Nice in the South of France are transformed into a simple, yet elegant, soup by adding a hot garlic-infused stock.

SERVES 4

12 drained bottled anchovy fillets

30ml/2 tbsp milk

115g/4oz green beans, halved, cooked in boiling salted water for 2–3 minutes, drained and refreshed in cold water

4 plum tomatoes, peeled, halved and seeded

16 black olives, stoned

1 litre/1¾ pints/4 cups good vegetable stock

3 garlic cloves, crushed

30ml/2 tbsp lemon juice

15ml/1 tbsp olive oil

4 tuna steaks, about 75g/3oz each

small bunch of spring onions (scallions), shredded lengthways

handful of fresh basil leaves, shredded

salt and ground black pepper

fresh crusty bread, to serve

1 Soak the anchovies in the milk for 10 minutes. Cut the tomatoes into thin wedges. Wash the olives to remove any oil, then cut into quarters. Set all these prepared ingredients aside.

2 Bring the stock to the boil in a large, heavy-based saucepan. Add the garlic, reduce the heat and simmer for 10 minutes. Season the stock well and add the lemon juice.

3 Meanwhile, brush a griddle pan or frying pan with the oil and heat until very hot.

4 Season the tuna and cook for about 2 minutes each side. Do not overcook the tuna or it will become dry and tough.

5 Gently toss together the French beans, tomatoes, spring onions, anchovies, black olives and shredded basil leaves.

6 Put the seared tuna steaks into four bowls and pile the vegetable mixture on top. Carefully ladle the hot garlic stock around the ingredients. Serve hot, with some crusty bread.

Nutritional information per portion: Energy 578kcal/2408kJ; Protein 46.4g; Carbohydrate 15g, of which sugars 10.6g; Fat 37.5g, of which saturates 7.1g; Cholesterol 235mg; Calcium 127mg; Fibre 4.7g; Sodium 585mg.

Ancona fish soup

This Italian dish is actually a chunky and substantial stew. Traditionally, 13 different varieties of fish are used; their quality and freshness are the most important elements of the dish.

SERVES 4–6

60ml/4 tbsp extra virgin olive oil
1 onion, chopped
1 garlic clove, chopped
90ml/6 tbsp white or red wine vinegar
300g/11oz canned tomatoes, sieved
    (strained) or coarsely chopped
900g/2lb mixed whole fish, such as small
    monkfish, red mullet or snapper,
    whiting or scorpion fish
sea salt and ground black pepper
crusty bread, to serve

1 Put the oil in a very large pan, add the onion and garlic, and fry over medium heat for 5 minutes, or until soft.

2 Gradually add the vinegar, stirring constantly, until the sharp vinegar smell has disappeared.

3 Add the canned tomatoes, stir and simmer for 10 minutes.

4 Gradually add the fish, one at a time, starting with the largest.

5 Cook, stirring occasionally, for 30 minutes, until the fish is cooked through. Serve with crusty bread.

COOK'S TIP
When choosing your fish, avoid strongly flavoured oily types as this could overpower more delicate fish.

Nutritional information per portion: Energy 389kcal/1627kJ; Protein 27.4g; Carbohydrate 29g, of which sugars 4.8g; Fat 18.9g, of which saturates 2.8g; Cholesterol 68mg; Calcium 46mg; Fibre 2.7g; Sodium 207mg.

Vermouth soup with seared scallops

Seared scallops form an elegant tower in the centre of this crème de la crème *of fine soups.*
The caviar garnish is an attractive and delicious addition.

SERVES 4

25g/1oz/2 tbsp butter

5 shallots, sliced

300ml/½ pint/1¼ cups dry white wine

300ml/½ pint/1¼ cups vermouth

900ml/1½ pints/3¾ cups fish stock

300ml/½ pint/1¼ cups double (heavy)
  cream

300ml/½ pint/1¼ cups single (light)
  cream

15ml/1 tbsp olive oil

12 large scallops

salt and ground black pepper

15ml/1 tbsp caviar and snipped chives,
  to garnish

FOR THE ROCKET OIL

115g/4oz rocket (arugula) leaves

120ml/4fl oz/½ cup olive oil

1 Prepare the rocket oil first. Process the rocket leaves and olive oil in a food processor for 1–2 minutes. Line a bowl with muslin and add the paste. Squeeze the muslin to extract the rocket-flavoured oil. Set aside.

2 Melt the butter in a large pan. Add the shallots and cook gently for 8–10 minutes, stirring, until soft but not browned.

3 Add the wine and vermouth and boil for 8–10 minutes, until reduced to a quarter in volume. Add the stock and bring back to the boil.

4 Boil until reduced by half. Pour in the double and single creams, and return to the boil. Reduce the heat and simmer for 12–15 minutes, until the soup is just thick enough to coat the back of a spoon. Strain the soup into a clean pan.

5 Brush the scallops with oil, and sear for 1 minute on each side in a hot frying pan. Reheat the soup, and season. Arrange three scallops in the centre of four soup plates. Ladle in the soup and top the scallops with a little caviar. Drizzle rocket oil over, then sprinkle with chives.

Nutritional information per portion: Energy 999kcal/4129kJ; Protein 26g; Carbohydrate 10g, of which sugars 6g; Fat 95g, of which saturates 43g; Cholesterol 213mg; Calcium 149 mg; Fibre 1g; Sodium 635mg.

Creamy crayfish soup

Crayfish are delicate and delicious; the sweetness of the meat gives a distinctive taste to this creamy soup. Paprika and lemon juice contrast well with the crayfish.

SERVES 4

50g/2oz/¼ cup unsalted butter
50g/2oz/1 cup plain (all-purpose) flour
700ml/1 pint 3½ fl oz/scant 3 cups fish
   or chicken stock
5ml/1 tsp paprika
1 egg yolk
120ml/4fl oz/½ cup double (heavy)
   cream
250g/9oz cooked crayfish meat
15ml/1 tbsp lemon juice
salt and ground black pepper
15ml/1 tbsp chopped fresh dill, to garnish

1 Melt the butter in a large heavy pan, stir in the flour to make a roux and cook gently over a low heat for 30 seconds, without colouring. Remove from the heat and gradually stir in the fish or chicken stock to form a smooth sauce.

2 Return the pan to the heat and, stirring all the time, cook until the sauce boils and thickens. Add the paprika and season to taste.

3 In a small bowl, mix the egg yolk and cream together, then stir into the soup and heat gently, taking care not to let the mixture boil or the soup will curdle.

4 Add the crayfish and lemon juice to the soup and heat gently. Adjust the seasoning if necessary. Pour the soup into individual serving bowls and serve hot, garnished with chopped dill.

Nutritional information per portion: Energy 348kcal/1444kJ; Protein 12.2g; Carbohydrate 10.9g, of which sugars 0.8g; Fat 28.8g, of which saturates 17g; Cholesterol 184mg; Calcium 65mg; Fibre 0.4g; Sodium 383mg.

Lobster and tomato soup

This luxurious lobster soup is for special occasions. The soup is equally good made with prawns, if you are feeling less extravagant. It is important to use lobster or prawns that are still in their shells, as they are needed to provide additional flavour to the soup.

SERVES 4

1 large cooked lobster or 500g/1¼lb/3 cups
  cooked prawns (shrimp)
25g/1oz/2 tbsp butter
30ml/2 tbsp finely chopped shallot
2 red (bell) peppers, seeded and chopped
2.5cm/1in fresh root ginger, finely chopped
1 clove garlic, finely chopped
60ml/4 tbsp brandy
30ml/2 tbsp tomato purée (paste)

1.25 litres/2¼ pints/5½ cups water
15ml/1 tbsp sherry vinegar
15ml/1 tbsp sugar
4 ripe tomatoes, skinned, seeded and chopped, or
  400g/14oz can tomatoes
juice of 1 lime
salt and ground black pepper
chopped fresh dill, to garnish

1 Remove the lobster or prawn meat from their shells, reserving the shells. Set the meat aside.

2 Melt the butter in a pan, add the shallots, peppers, ginger and garlic and cook for 5 minutes. Add the shells tot he pan and cook gently for a further 10 minutes.

3 Add the brandy to the pan and set alight. Stir in the tomato purée. Add the water, season lightly with salt and pepper, and bring to the boil. Lower the heat and simmer very gently for 40 minutes.

4 Strain the mixture into a clean pan. Add the vinegar, sugar, tomatoes and lime juice to taste, and taste to check the seasonings, adding salt and pepper only if necessary.

5 Divide the lobster or prawn meat between four individual serving bowls. Bring the soup to the boil, then pour over the shellfish. Serve, garnished with chopped dill.

Nutritional information per portion: Energy 275kcal/1155kJ; Protein 29.6g; Carbohydrate 14.1g, of which sugars 13.5g; Fat 7.8g, of which saturates 3.7g; Cholesterol 151mg; Calcium 99mg; Fibre 2.6g; Sodium 479mg.

Saffron-flavoured mussel soup

There's a fragrant taste of the sea off the Spanish coast in this creamy soup filled with the jet black shells of plump mussels. You only need a litte saffron to add colour and flavour.

SERVES 4

1.5kg/3–3½ lb fresh mussels
600 ml/1 pint /2½ cups white wine
a few fresh parsley stalks
50g/2oz/¼ cup butter
2 leeks, finely chopped
2 celery sticks, finely chopped
1 carrot, chopped
2 garlic cloves, chopped
a large pinch of saffron threads
600ml/1 pint /2½ cups double (heavy)
   cream
3 tomatoes, peeled, seeded and chopped
salt and ground black pepper
30 ml/2 tbsp chopped fresh chives,
   to garnish

1 Scrub the mussels and pull away the beards. Put them in a large pan with the wine and parsley stalks. Cover, bring to the boil and cook for 4–5 minutes, shaking the pan occasionally, until the mussels have opened. Discard any mussels that fail to open.

2 Drain the mussels over a large bowl, reserving the cooking liquid. When they are cool enough to handle, remove about half of the cooked mussels from their shells. Set aside with the remaining mussels in their shells. Strain and reserve the cooking liquid.

3 Melt the butter in a large pan and add the leeks, celery, carrot and garlic. Cook for 5 minutes until soft.

4 Add the strained stock to the pan and cook over a high heat for 8–10 minutes to reduce slightly. Strain again into a clean pan, add the saffron and cook for 1 minute.

5 Add the cream and bring back to the boil. Season well. Add all the mussels and the tomatoes, and heat gently to warm through. Ladle the soup into four warmed shallow soup bowls, then garnish with the chopped chives and serve.

Nutritional information per portion: Energy 441kcal/1825kJ; Protein 9.6g; Carbohydrate 3.1g, of which sugars 3.1g; Fat 39.1g, of which saturates 23.9g; Cholesterol 116mg; Calcium 137mg; Fibre 0.6g; Sodium 156mg.

Chilli clam broth

This soup, of succulent clams in a tasty stock, could not be easier to prepare. Popular in coastal areas of Colombia, it makes the perfect lunch on a hot summer's day.

SERVES 6

30ml/2 tbsp olive oil

1 onion, finely chopped

3 garlic cloves, crushed

2 fresh red chillies, seeded and finely chopped

250ml/8fl oz/1 cup dry white wine

400ml/14fl oz can plum tomatoes, drained

1 large potato, about 250g/9oz, peeled and diced

400ml/14fl oz/1²⁄₃ cups fish stock

1.3kg/3lb fresh clams

15ml/1 tbsp chopped fresh coriander (cilantro)

15ml/1 tbsp chopped fresh flat leaf parsley

salt

lime wedges, to garnish

1 Heat the oil in a pan. Add the onion and sauté for 5 minutes over a low heat. Stir in the garlic and chillies and cook for 2 minutes more. Pour in the wine and bring to the boil, then simmer for 2 minutes.

2 Add the tomatoes, diced potato and stock. Bring back to the boil, then cover and lower the heat to a gentle simmer.

3 Season with salt and cook for 15 minutes, until the potatoes are beginning to break up and the tomatoes have made a rich sauce.

4 Meanwhile, wash the clams thoroughly under cold running water. Gently tap any that are open, and discard if they do not close.

5 Add the clams to the soup, cover the pan and cook for about 3–4 minutes, or until the clams have opened, then stir in the chopped herbs. Season with salt to taste.

6 Throw away any clams that have failed to open. Ladle the soup into warmed bowls. Offer the lime wedges separately, to be squeezed over the soup before eating.

Nutritional information per portion: Energy 290kcal/1217kJ; Protein 36.2g; Carbohydrate 14.1g, of which sugars 3.5g; Fat 7.2g, of which saturates 1.3g; Cholesterol 145mg; Calcium 184mg; Fibre 1.5g; Sodium 151mg.

Three-fish mousse

This rich and creamy mousse is flavoured with lemon and dill. It makes a perfect start to a special meal, as it is made in advance, has a lovely flavour, and looks absolutely stunning.

SERVES 6–8

15ml/1 tbsp oil
450g/1lb cod fillet, skinned
1 bay leaf
1 slice lemon
6 black peppercorns
275g/10oz smoked trout, thinly sliced
60ml/4 tbsp cold water
15g/1/2 oz powdered gelatine
175g/6oz cooked peeled prawns (shrimp), halved

300ml/1/2 pint/11/4 cups sour cream
225g/8oz/1 cup cream cheese
30ml/2 tbsp chopped fresh dill
juice of 1 lemon
3 drops Tabasco sauce
salt and ground black pepper
sprigs of fresh herbs, such as parsley or dill,
    and 6–8 lemon wedges, to garnish

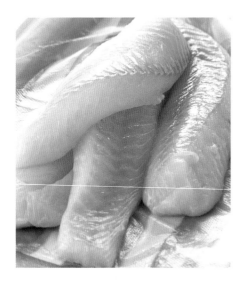

1 Brush a 1.2 litre/2 pint/5 cup ring mould with the oil. Place the cod, bay leaf, lemon slice and peppercorns in a pan. Cover with cold water and bring to simmering point. Poach for 10–15 minutes, or until the fish flakes when tested with a fork.

2 Line the oiled ring mould with overlapping slices of smoked trout, leaving plenty hanging over the edge.

3 Remove the cod from the pan with a fish slice or metal spatula. Chop the cod into chunks and put it in a large bowl. Place the measured cold water in a small heatproof bowl and sprinkle the gelatine over the surface. Leave for 5 minutes, until spongy, then place the bowl over a pan of hot water. Stir until the gelatine has dissolved. Leave to cool slightly.

4 Add the prawns, sour cream, cream cheese and dill to the cod. Add the lemon juice and Tabasco sauce. Mash all together. Season to taste. Fold the gelatine into the fish mixture, then spoon into the ring mould and smooth the top with a spoon.

5 Fold the overhanging edges of the trout over the mousse. Cover and chill in the refrigerator for 2 hours. Run a round-bladed knife around the edge of the mousse, invert a plate on top and turn both over. Shake until the mousse drops out on to the plate. Garnish with the herbs and lemon and serve.

Nutritional information per portion: Nutritional information per portion: Energy 334kcal/1386kJ; Protein 25g; Carbohydrate 2g, of which sugars 2g; Fat 25g, of which saturates 14g; Cholesterol 161mg; Calcium 101mg; Fibre 0g; Sodium 506mg.

Three-fish terrine

An ideal appetizer when entertaining, this striped terrine uses haddock, salmon and turbot and is slowly baked in the oven. Serve with a small salad, brown bread or Melba toast and butter.

SERVES 8–10

450g/1lb young spinach leaves, washed
350–450g/12oz–1lb haddock, cod or
   other white fish, skinned and chopped
3 eggs
115g/4oz/2 cups fresh breadcrumbs
300ml/½ pint/1¼ cups fromage blanc
   or low-fat cream cheese
a little freshly grated nutmeg
350–450g/12oz–1lb salmon fillet and
   350–450g/12oz–1lb fresh turbot fillet,
   skinned, bones removed, and cut into
   long thin strips
oil, for greasing
salt and ground black pepper
lemon wedges, Melba toast and rocket
   (arugula), to serve

1 Preheat the oven to 160°C/325°F/Gas 3. Dry-fry the spinach, shaking the pan, until wilted. Drain and squeeze out the water.

2 Put the spinach into a food processor with the haddock, eggs, breadcrumbs, fromage blanc or cream cheese, salt, pepper and nutmeg. Process until smooth.

3 Oil a 900g/2lb loaf tin (pan) and line the base with baking parchment. Make layers of the spinach mixture and the strips of salmon and turbot, starting and finishing with spinach.

4 Press down and cover with oiled baking parchment. Prick a few holes in it, put the terrine into a roasting pan and pour boiling water in to two-thirds of the way up the sides.

5 Bake in the preheated oven for 1–1½ hours, or until risen, firm and set. Leave to cool, then chill well.

6 To serve the terrine, ease a sharp knife down all four sides to loosen, place a flat serving dish on top and turn upside down so the terrine slides out. Slice and serve with lemon, Melba toast and rocket.

Nutritional information per portion: Energy 290Kcal/1216kJ; Protein 32.5g; Carbohydrate 13.7g, of which sugars 2.8g; Fat 12.1g, of which saturates 3.9g; Cholesterol 112mg; Calcium 203mg; Fibre 1.5g; Sodium 306mg.

Smoked mackerel pâté

The south-west coast of England is known for its smoked fish, especially freshly caught mackerel. This modern recipe is quick and easy, involves no cooking and is very versatile.

SERVES 4–6

225g/8oz/1 cup crème fraîche or Greek
   (US strained plain) yogurt
finely grated rind of ½ lemon
a few sprigs of parsley
225g/8oz smoked mackerel fillets
5–10ml/1–2 tsp horseradish sauce
1 tbsp lemon juice, or to taste
ground black pepper
crusty bread, hot toast or crisp plain
   crackers, to serve
lemon wedges, to serve

1 Put the crème fraîche or yogurt and lemon rind into a food processor. Add the sprigs of parsley.

2 Flake the mackerel, discarding the skin and removing any bones. Add the flaked fish to the blender. Blend on a medium speed until the mixture is almost smooth.

3 Add the horseradish sauce and lemon juice and blend briefly. Season with ground black pepper.

4 Divide the pâté equally among individual serving dishes.

5 Cover the dishes with clear film (plastic wrap) and refrigerate until required, or for a minimum of 2 hours.

6 Garnish with parsley and serve with crusty bread, hot toast or crackers and lemon wedges for squeezing over.

Nutritional information per portion: Energy 344kcal/1421kJ; Protein 10.7g; Carbohydrate 0.5g, of which sugars 0.4g; Fat 33.3g, of which saturates 14.3g; Cholesterol 88mg; Calcium 57mg; Fibre 0.1g; Sodium 518mg.

Lemon-marinated salmon with horseradish

For a celebratory meal there is no finer fish than salmon. Curing it yourself in a blanket of salt and sugar – the preparation method known as gravad lax – is simple and makes a tasty appetizer.

SERVES 8–10

1kg/2¼ lb fresh salmon fillet, skin on, bones removed with tweezers
75g/3oz/⅓ cup coarse salt
25g/1oz/2 tbsp sugar
10ml/2 tsp ground white pepper
30ml/2 tbsp fresh lemon juice
105ml/7 tbsp chopped fresh dill
½ lemon, thinly sliced, plus extra to garnish

FOR THE DRESSING
250ml/8fl oz/1 cup sour cream
30ml/2 tbsp double (heavy) cream
45ml/3 tbsp prepared creamed horseradish sauce, or to taste
45ml/3 tbsp chopped fresh dill
salt and ground white pepper
fresh dill sprigs, to garnish

1 Line a roasting pan with foil, leaving sides and ends overlapping. Nick the salmon skin to allow the salt and seasonings to penetrate, then cut the fillet in half.

2 Mix the salt, sugar and pepper in a bowl. Place one piece of salmon, skin side down, in the lined pan. Drizzle with lemon juice, rub with half the salt mixture, and sprinkle over half the dill. Arrange the lemon slices over the fish. Rub the second fillet with the remaining salt mixture and remaining dill.

3 Carefully lift the second fillet and place it on top of the fillet in the pan, skin side up.

4 Wrap tightly in the foil and weight with a heavy pan. Refrigerate for 48 hours, turning the fish twice daily. The salmon will be cured when it turns a bright red and the edges are slightly dry. To serve, cut the salmon from the skin in very thin slices.

5 Mix the dressing ingredients together and serve with the salmon, garnished with dill sprigs.

Nutritional information per portion: Energy 479kcal/1981kJ; Protein 26.2g; Carbohydrate 0.4g, of which sugars 0.3g; Fat 40.4g, of which saturates 6.4g; Cholesterol 113mg; Calcium 35mg; Fibre 0g; Sodium 169mg.

Brandade of salt cod

There are many versions of this creamy French salt cod purée: some contain mashed potatoes, others truffles. Serve the brandade with crispbread or warmed crusty bread.

SERVES 6

200g/7oz salt cod, soaked in cold water
   for 24 hours, changing the
   water frequently
250ml/8fl oz/1 cup extra virgin olive oil
4 garlic cloves, crushed
250ml/8fl oz/1 cup double (heavy) or
   whipping cream
crispbread or crusty bread, to serve

COOK'S TIP
*When buying salt cod, the best pieces
are from the middle of the fish rather
than the tail end. Look for pieces that are
already the size you require, as it is very
difficult to cut up.*

1 Drain the fish well and cut into pieces, place in a shallow pan and pour in enough cold water to cover. Heat the water until it is simmering and poach the fish for 8 minutes, until it is just cooked. Drain the fish, then remove the skin and bones.

2 Combine the extra virgin olive oil and crushed garlic cloves in a small pan and heat gently. In another pan, heat the double cream until it just starts to simmer.

3 Put the cod into a food processor, process it briefly, then gradually add alternate amounts of the garlic-flavoured olive oil and cream, while continuing to process the mixture to the consistency of mashed potato. Season to taste with ground black pepper, no more salt is needed.

4 Scoop the brandade into a serving bowl or on to individual serving plates and serve with crispbread or warmed crusty bread.

Nutritional information per portion: Energy 467kcal/1927kJ; Protein 11.7g; Carbohydrate 1.1g, of which sugars 1.1g; Fat 46.2g, of which saturates 14.8g; Cholesterol 63mg; Calcium 32mg; Fibre 0g; Sodium 144mg.

Marinated herrings

This appetizer is much enjoyed in Scandinavian countries. Sweet-and-sour and lightly spiced, it is also delicious for Sunday brunch served with fresh rye or pumpernickel bread.

SERVES 4–6

2–3 very fresh herrings, filleted
1 onion, sliced
juice of 1½ lemons
30ml/2 tbsp white wine vinegar
25ml/1½ tbsp sugar
10–15 black peppercorns
10–15 allspice berries
1.5ml/¼ tsp mustard seeds
3 bay leaves, torn
salt

1 Soak the herring fillets in cold water for 5 minutes, then drain. Pour over enough water to cover them and soak for 2–3 hours, then drain. Again, pour over water to cover the herrings and leave to soak overnight in a cool place.

2 Rinse the herrings well, under cold running water, both inside and out. Cut each fish into bitesize pieces, then place the pieces in a glass bowl or shallow dish.

3 Sprinkle the sliced onion over the fish, then add the lemon juice, vinegar, sugar, peppercorns, allspice, mustard seeds, bay leaves and salt.

4 Add enough water to just cover. Cover the bowl with clear film (plastic wrap) and chill in the refrigerator for about 2 days to allow the flavours to blend thoroughly before serving. The herrings will keep for up to 1 week in the refrigerator.

Nutritional information per portion: Energy 94kcal/393kJ; Protein 7.7g; Carbohydrate 3.4g, of which sugars 3.2g; Fat 5.6g, of which saturates 1.4g; Cholesterol 21mg; Calcium 29mg; Fibre 0.1g; Sodium 52mg

Marinated anchovies

This is one of the simplest ways to prepare these tiny fish because no cooking is required. Marinating is particularly associated with anchovies, which tend to lose their freshness quickly.

SERVES 4

225g/8oz fresh anchovies, heads and
    tails removed, and split open along
    the belly
juice of 3 lemons
30ml/2 tbsp extra virgin olive oil
2 garlic cloves, finely chopped
15ml/1 tbsp chopped fresh parsley
flaked sea salt
fresh crusty bread, to serve

1 First you need to debone the fish; turn the anchovies on their bellies, and press down with your thumb.

2 Using the tip of a small, sharp knife, carefully remove the backbones from the flattened fish. Arrange them skin side down in a single layer on a large, flat plate.

3 Squeeze two-thirds of the lemon juice over the fish and sprinkle them with the salt.

4 Cover and leave to stand for up to 24 hours, basting occasionally with the juices, until the flesh is white and no longer translucent.

5 Transfer the anchovies to a serving plate and drizzle with the olive oil and the remaining lemon juice.

6 Scatter the chopped garlic and parsley over the fish, then cover with clear film (plastic wrap) and chill until ready to serve with bread.

Nutritional information per portion: Energy 144kcal/597kJ; Protein 11.7g; Carbohydrate 0.1g, of which sugars 0.1g; Fat 10.7g, of which saturates 2.3g; Cholesterol 0mg; Calcium 55mg; Fibre 0.2g; Sodium 69mg.

Sardines in onion and tomato marinade

This is a traditional Portuguese dish. The basic marinade consists of onion, garlic, bay leaves and good-quality wine vinegar, to which tomatoes or other vegetables may be added.

SERVES 4–6

12 sardines, cleaned

plain (all-purpose) flour, for dusting

150ml/¼ pint/⅔ cup olive oil

2 onions, halved and finely diced

3 bay leaves

2 garlic cloves, chopped

150ml/¼ pint/⅔ cup white wine
    vinegar

2 ripe tomatoes, diced

sea salt

crusty bread, to serve

1 Dust the sardines with flour. Heat 75ml/5 tbsp of the olive oil in a heavy frying pan. Add the sardines, in batches, and cook over a medium heat, for about 1 minute each side. Remove with a slotted spatula and drain on kitchen paper.

2 In a clean pan, cook the onions, bay leaves and garlic with the rest of the olive oil over a low heat, stirring occasionally, for about 5 minutes, until softened. Add the vinegar and the tomatoes, and season with sea salt to taste.

3 Return the sardines to the pan. If they are not completely covered, add a little water or some more vinegar. Cook for a few minutes then transfer the mixture to a deep plate, allow to cool and leave to marinate in the refrigerator overnight, or for at least 6 hours. Serve with bread.

COOK'S TIPS
You can leave the sardines marinating for up to 3–5 days. Don't be sparing with the vinegar, as it will all be absorbed, and help to offset the oily flavour of the sardines.

Nutritional information per portion: Energy 335kcal/1392kJ; Protein 21.2g; Carbohydrate 4.3g, of which sugars 1.1g; Fat 26g, of which saturates 5.1g; Cholesterol 0mg; Calcium 92mg; Fibre 0.5g; Sodium 123mg.

Fried whitebait with cayenne pepper

For the perfect beach snack, try these crisp, spicy, bitesize fish with a squeeze of lime. They can be eaten as they are or served with a simple tomato and onion salad dressed with lemon juice.

SERVES 4

50g/2oz/½ cup plain (all-purpose) flour
1.5ml/¼ tsp cayenne pepper
250g/9oz whitebait
vegetable oil, for deep-frying
salt and ground black pepper
lime wedges, to serve

COOK'S TIP
Small fresh anchovies are also delicious cooked whole in this way. Try as part of a mixed seafood platter using whitebait, anchovies and prawns (shrimp), served with grilled salmon kebabs.

1 Sift the flour and cayenne pepper into a large bowl. Season with salt and ground black pepper.

2 Thoroughly coat the whitebait in the seasoned flour, then shake off any excess flour and make sure the whitebait are separate. Do this in batches, placing the coated fish on a plate ready for frying. Pour oil to a depth of 5cm/2in into a deep pan.

3 Heat the oil until very hot, then add a batch of whitebait and fry for 2–3 minutes until golden. Remove from the pan with a slotted spoon and drain on kitchen paper. Repeat with the remaining whitebait.

4 Pile the fried whitebait on a plate, season generously with salt and serve immediately, with the lime wedges squeezed over.

Nutritional information per portion: Energy 722kcal/2989kJ; Protein 13g; Carbohydrate 13.1g, of which sugars 5.1g; Fat 32.8g, of which saturates 3.4g; Cholesterol 0mg; Calcium 526mg; Fibre 2g; Sodium 191mg.

Fried squid with salt and pepper

Cooking squid couldn't be simpler. Salt and pepper are used to season, and that is all that is needed. The way the squid is cooked in this recipe is traditionally Chinese, but it is a Vietnamese favourite too. Ideal snack and finger food, the tender squid can be served on its own, with noodles, or – as it is eaten in the streets of Saigon – with a baguette and chillies.

SERVES 4

450g/1lb baby or medium squid
30ml/2 tbsp coarse salt
15ml/1 tbsp ground black pepper
50g/2oz/½ cup rice flour or cornflour
   (cornstarch)

vegetable or sesame oil, for frying
2 limes, cut into wedges

1 Prepare the squid by gently but firmly pulling the head away from the body. Sever the tentacles from the head and trim them, discarding the beak and the head. Remove and reserve the ink sac.

2 Reach inside the body sac and pull out the 'quill' or backbone, then clean the squid inside and out, removing any skin. Rinse well in cold water.

3 Using a sharp knife, slice the squid into rings and pat them dry. Put them on a dish with the tentacles.

4 Combine the salt and pepper with the rice flour or cornflour in a large bowl, add the squid rings and tentacles to the bowl and toss well, making sure they are evenly coated.

5 Heat the oil in a wok or heavy pan for deep-frying. Cook the squid in batches, until the rings turn crisp and golden. Drain on kitchen paper and serve with lime wedges to squeeze over.

COOK'S TIP
To use the ink sac, put it in a bowl and pierce with a knife. Use the ink, diluted with water, to flavour and colour homemade pasta and risotto.

Nutritional information per portion: Energy 339Kcal/1405kJ; Protein 14g; Carbohydrate 5g, of which sugars 0g; Fat 29g, of which saturates 4g; Cholesterol 146mg; Calcium 70mg; Fibre 0g; Sodium 1.4g.

Anchovy fritters

This unusual batter is made with yeast, which makes it really light and crisp. The fritters make a lovely tasty snack, especially when served with plenty of dry white wine.

SERVES 12

1kg/2¼lb/9 cups plain (all-purpose) flour
120ml/4fl oz/½ cup hand-hot water with 50g/2oz fresh (compressed) yeast crumbled in and dissolved
1.5ml/¼ tsp salt
300g/11oz salted anchovies, rinsed, boned and dried and roughly chopped
sunflower oil or light olive oil, for deep-frying

1 Put the flour into a bowl and make a well in the centre.

2 Pour the yeast and water mixture into the well in the flour. Using your hands, mix the water into the flour, adding more water if required to make a sticky, stringy mass. Be careful not to add too much liquid.

3 Knead the batter by beating with your hands in a circular motion for about 30 minutes. Beat in the salt. Cover the bowl with a cloth and leave the batter to rise at room temperature for 3–4 hours.

4 Heat the oil in a large pan to 180°C/350°F or until a small cube of bread, dropped into the oil, browns in about 45 seconds.

5 Scoop up about a tablespoonful of batter and stretch it slightly with your fingers. Tuck a few pieces of anchovy inside, seal, and drop the dough into the hot oil.

6 Fry in batches, for 4–6 minutes, until the fritters rise to the surface and turn crisp and golden, then lift them out and drain on kitchen paper. Serve straight away.

Nutritional information per portion: Energy 416kcal/1753kJ; Protein 14.5g; Carbohydrate 64.9g, of which sugars 1.3g; Fat 12.7g, of which saturates 2.1g; Cholesterol 0mg; Calcium 141mg; Fibre 2.6g; Sodium 34.6mg.

Goat's cheese and trout toasties

These little rounds are packed full of flavour – the goat's cheese and smoked trout combine beautifully to make a delicious snack suitable for any time of the day.

SERVES 4

8 thick slices of white bread
30ml/2 tbsp olive oil
5ml/1 tsp fresh thyme leaves
20ml/4 tsp pesto
50g/2oz smoked trout slices
4 round goat's cheese slices
salt and ground black pepper
cherry tomatoes and fresh basil, to serve

COOK'S TIP

For a milder flavour, use rounds of under-ripe Brie or Camembert cheese in place of the goat's cheese.

1 Preheat the oven to 200°C/400°F/Gas 6. Using a pastry cutter that is slightly larger than the goat's cheese rounds, cut a circle from each slice of bread.

2 Brush the bread rounds with a little olive oil, scatter with a few thyme leaves and season well. Place the bread rounds on a baking sheet and bake for 5 minutes or until crisp and a light golden colour. Remove the rounds from the oven.

3 Spread pesto over half the rounds. Divide the smoked trout among the pesto-topped bread, top with the cheese rounds and season well with black pepper. Top the cheese with the remaining bread circles.

4 Bake the toasties in the oven for 5 minutes more, until the cheese has just started to soften. Remove from the oven and serve immediately with the cherry tomatoes and fresh basil.

Nutritional information per portion: Energy 349kcal/1467kJ; Protein 13g; Carbohydrate 41g, of which sugars 3g; Fat 16g, of which saturates 4g; Cholesterol 22mg; Calcium 249mg; Fibre 3g; Sodium 629mg.

Langoustines with saffron and tomato

The best langoustines come from the west coast of Scotland, and are also known as Dublin Bay prawns or Norway lobster. They taste more like King prawns or shrimp than lobster.

SERVES 4

5ml/1 tsp sea salt
20 live langoustines (jumbo shrimp)
1 onion, chopped
15ml/1 tbsp olive oil
a pinch of saffron threads
120ml/4fl oz/½ cup white wine
450g/1lb ripe fresh or canned tomatoes, roughly chopped
chopped fresh flat leaf parsley, to garnish
salt and ground black pepper

1 Bring a large pan of water to the boil, add the salt and plunge the shellfish into the pan. Let the water return to the boil, then transfer the shellfish to a colander to cool.

2 Shell the langoustines or prawns and reserve four heads with two claws each. Keep the rest of the shells, heads and claws to make stock for the sauce.

3 Heat a large pan and add 15ml/ 1 tbsp olive oil. Gently fry the onion until soft. Stir in the saffron threads. Then add the shellfish debris, including the heads and pincers.

4 Add the wine to the pan and then the tomatoes. Simmer to soften the tomatoes, about 5 minutes. Add a little water if it looks dry.

5 Strain into a clean pan through a sieve (strainer), pushing the debris to get all the moisture out. The resulting sauce should be light in texture; if it is too thick, add some water. Check the seasoning.

6 Add the langoustines or prawns and warm for a few minutes. Serve in soup plates, garnished with the reserved langoustine or prawn heads, and scattered with parsley.

Nutritional information per portion: Energy 107kcal/449kJ; Protein 9.8g; Carbohydrate 4.9g, of which sugars 4.5g; Fat 3.4g, of which saturates 0.6g; Cholesterol 98mg; Calcium 54mg; Fibre 1.3g; Sodium 598mg.

Saffron mussels with white wine

Mussels are quick and easy to cook, and they stay deliciously moist. The saffron adds a lovely pungent flavour as well as its distinctive yellow colour to the creamy sauce.

SERVES 4

1kg/2¼lb mussels in their shells
few threads of saffron, soaked in 15ml/
    1 tbsp boiling water
    for 15 minutes
25g/1oz/2 tbsp butter
2 shallots, finely chopped
2 garlic cloves, finely chopped
200ml/7fl oz/scant 1 cup dry white wine
60ml/4 tbsp double (heavy) cream or
    crème fraîche
30ml/2 tbsp chopped fresh parsley
salt and ground black pepper
French bread, to serve

1 Scrub the mussels and pull off the beards. Discard any open mussels that don't close when tapped.

2 Melt the butter in a large pan. Add the shallots and garlic and cook gently for 5 minutes, to soften. Stir in the wine and saffron threads and water, and bring to the boil.

3 Add the mussels and cover. Cook for 3–4 minutes, shaking the pan occasionally, until the mussels open.

4 Using a slotted spoon, transfer the mussels to four warmed serving bowls (discard any mussels that have not opened).

5 Mix the cream or crème fraîche and parsley into the cooking liquid, reheat gently but do not boil, and season to taste.

6 Pour the cooking liquid over the mussels and serve with bread.

Nutritional information per portion: Energy 224Kcal/935kJ; Protein 13.5g; Carbohydrate 1.8g, of which sugars 1.4g; Fat 14.7g, of which saturates 8.5g; Cholesterol 64mg; Calcium 164mg; Fibre 0.2g; Sodium 201mg.

Mussels with a parsley crust

Here mussels are grilled with a deliciously fragrant topping of Parmesan cheese, garlic and parsley, which helps to prevent the mussels from becoming overcooked.

SERVES 4

450g/1lb fresh mussels, scrubbed and
   with beards removed
45ml/3 tbsp water
15ml/1 tbsp melted butter
15ml/1 tbsp olive oil
45ml/3 tbsp freshly grated Parmesan
   cheese
30ml/2 tbsp chopped fresh parsley, plus
   extra to garnish
2 garlic cloves, finely chopped
2.5ml/½ tsp coarsely ground black
   pepper
crusty bread, to serve

1 Sharply tap any open mussels and discard any that fail to close or that have broken shells.

2 Place the mussels in a large pan and add the water. Cover the pan with a tight-fitting lid and steam for about 5 minutes, until opened.

3 Drain the mussels and discard any that remain closed. Carefully snap off the top shell from each mussel, leaving the flesh still attached to the bottom shell.

4 Balance the shells in a flameproof dish, packing them together so they stay level. Preheat the grill (broiler) to high. Put the melted butter, olive oil, Parmesan cheese, parsley, garlic and pepper in a small bowl and mix.

5 Divide the cheese and garlic mixture between each mussel and press down. Grill (broil) the mussels for about 2 minutes, or until they are sizzling. Serve in their shells, garnished with chopped parsley, and with bread to mop up the juices.

Nutritional information per portion: Energy 110kcal/456kJ; Protein 5.4g; Carbohydrate 0.3g, of which sugars 0.3g; Fat 9.7g, of which saturates 4.7g; Cholesterol 21mg; Calcium 165mg; Fibre 0.6g; Sodium 156mg.

Lemon, chilli and herb steamed razor clams

Razor clams make a wonderful appetizer for a special meal. Here they are lightly steamed and tossed in a fragrant Italian-style dressing of chilli, lemon, garlic and parsley.

SERVES 4

12 razor clams
90–120ml/6–8 tbsp extra virgin olive oil
finely grated rind and juice of 1 small
    lemon
2 garlic cloves, very finely grated
1 red chilli, seeded and very finely
    chopped
60ml/4 tbsp chopped flat leaf parsley
salt and ground black pepper
mixed salad leaves and crusty bread,
    to serve

1 Wash the razor clams well in plently of cold running water. Drain and arrange half the clams in a steamer, with the hinge side downward.

2 Pour 5cm/2in water into a wok and bring to the boil. Carefully balance the steamer over the water and cover tightly. Steam for 3–4 minutes, or until the clams have fully opened. Remove the clams from the wok.

3 Keep the clams warm while you steam the rest in the same way.

4 In a bowl, mix together the olive oil, grated lemon rind and juice, garlic, red chilli and chopped flat leaf parsley. Season well with salt and pepper.

5 Spoon the mixture over the steamed clams and serve immediately with a crisp mixed-leaf salad and crusty bread.

Nutritional information per portion: Energy 188kcal/775kJ; Protein 6.1g; Carbohydrate 2.9g, of which sugars 0.5g; Fat 16.9g, of which saturates 2.4g; Cholesterol 20mg; Calcium 47mg; Fibre 1.1g; Sodium 364mg.

Steamed oysters with zesty salsa

A plate of lightly steamed fresh oysters makes a delicious appetizer for a special occasion. The fresh, zesty, aromatic salsa complements their delicate flavour and texture perfectly.

SERVES 4

12–16 oysters, scrubbed under cold
    running water
30ml/2 tbsp sunflower oil
1 garlic clove, crushed
15ml/1 tbsp light soy sauce
sea salt, to serve

FOR THE SALSA
1 ripe plum tomato, seeded and diced
1/2 small cucumber, diced
1/4 small red onion, finely diced
15ml/1 tbsp very finely chopped
    coriander (cilantro)
1 small red chilli, seeded and very finely
    chopped
juice of 1–2 limes
salt and ground black pepper

1 First prepare the salsa. Place the tomato, cucumber and onion in a bowl with the coriander and red chilli. Add the lime juice and season to taste. Set aside.

2 Wrap one hand in a clean dish towel and hold an oyster with the cupped shell down and the narrow hinged end toward you. Using an oyster knife or a strong knife with a short, blunt blade, push the point of the knife into the gap between the shells until the hinge breaks. Pull up the top shell.

3 Sever the muscle that joins the oyster to the shell and lift off the top shell. Repeat with all the oysters and arrange in a bamboo steamer (using several tiers if necessary).

4 Mix together the sunflower oil, garlic and soy sauce, and spoon over the oysters.

5 Cover and steam the oysters over simmering water for 2–3 minutes, or until slightly firm. Arrange on a bed of sea salt, top each oyster with salsa and serve.

Nutritional information per portion: Energy 82kcal/339kJ; Protein 4.5g; Carbohydrate 2.4g, of which sugars 1.3g; Fat 6.1g, of which saturates 0.8g; Cholesterol 21mg; Calcium 60mg; Fibre 0.4g; Sodium 461mg.

Steamed scallops with ginger

Serve these juicy, fragrant scallops with their subtly spiced flavour as an indulgent starter for a special occasion. For the best results, use the freshest scallops you can find.

SERVES 8

24 king scallops in their shells, cleaned

15ml/1 tbsp very finely shredded fresh root ginger

5ml/1 tsp very finely chopped garlic

1 large red chilli, seeded and very finely chopped

15ml/1 tbsp light soy sauce

15ml/1 tbsp Chinese rice wine

a few drops of sesame oil

2–3 spring onions (scallions), very finely shredded

15ml/1 tbsp very finely chopped fresh chives

1 Remove the scallops from their shells, then remove the membrane and hard white muscle from each one. Arrange the scallops on two plates. Rinse and dry the shells.

2 Fill two woks with 5cm/2in water and place a trivet in the base of each one. Bring to the boil.

3 Mix together the ginger, garlic, chilli, soy sauce, rice wine, sesame oil, spring onions and chives and spoon over the scallops.

4 Lower a plate of scallops into each of the woks. Turn the heat to low, cover and steam for 10–12 minutes, or until just cooked through. Divide the scallops among eight of the reserved shells and serve straight away.

COOK'S TIP

An easy way to open scallops is to place them on a baking sheet in an oven preheated to 160°C/325°F/Gas 3 for a few moments, until they gape sufficiently to ease the shells apart.

Nutritional information per portion: Energy 157kcal/664kJ; Protein 29g; Carbohydrate 5g, of which sugars 1g; Fat 3g, of which saturates 1g; Cholesterol 56mg; Calcium 41mg; Fibre 0g; Sodium 432mg.

Asparagus and smoked fish salad

In spite of its long list of ingredients, this is deceptively simple to make, with a sophisticated mix of white and green asparagus. Begin well in advance, as the marinating takes up to 2 hours.

SERVES 4

600g/1lb 6oz white asparagus, peeled and cut into 1cm/½ in pieces

300g/11oz green asparagus, peeled and cut into 1cm/½ in pieces

20ml/4 tsp sunflower oil

1 onion, finely sliced

15ml/1 tbsp cider vinegar

15ml/1 tbsp apple juice

10 cherry tomatoes, halved

200g/7oz smoked salmon

200g/7oz flaked kiln-smoked salmon

salt, ground white pepper, sugar

FOR THE GREEN SAUCE

200ml/7fl oz/scant 1 cup yogurt

200ml/7fl oz/scant 1 cup sour cream

5ml/1 tsp Dijon mustard

juice of ½ lemon

2 hard-boiled eggs, separated into yolk and white

10ml/2 tsp sunflower oil

150g/5oz parsley and chives, chopped

salt, ground white pepper, sugar

1 Cook the asparagus in separate pans for 4–5 minutes or until just tender. Drain and refresh under cold running water. Put the white asparagus in a bowl and set the green aside.

2 Heat the oil in a frying pan over medium heat and cook the onions for 2 minutes. Add the vinegar and apple juice and season with salt, pepper and sugar. Bring to the boil and remove from the heat. Pour the hot dressing over the white asparagus. Stir in the tomatoes and marinate for 1–2 hours.

3 To make the green sauce, mix the yogurt with the sour cream, mustard and lemon juice and season to taste with salt, pepper and sugar. Mash the egg yolk with a fork and blend with the oil, then stir into the yogurt and cream mixture. Finely dice the egg white and stir it into the dressing, with the herbs.

4 Remove the asparagus and tomatoes from the dressing and toss with the green asparagus. Arrange the salad on serving plates, together with the two types of fish. Serve the sauce on the side.

Nutritional information per portion: Energy 644kcal/2664kJ; Protein 34.2g; Carbohydrate 13.4g, of which sugars 12.5g; Fat 50.9g, of which saturates 14.4g; Cholesterol 230mg; Calcium 319mg; Fibre 6.1g; Sodium 864mg.

Octopus salad

A tangy octopus appetizer is often served at Christmas in Portugal. Eaten cold with plenty of parsley, the octopus flavour is less intense. This will serve four as a substantial appetizer.

SERVES 4–8

1 uncooked octopus, weighing
   2–3kg/4½–6½ lb, cleaned, trimmed
   and beak removed
105ml/7 tbsp olive oil
30–45ml/2–3 tbsp white wine vinegar
1 onion, finely chopped
a bunch of parsley, chopped

FOR THE STOCK

2 onions, quartered
1 leek, chopped
3 garlic cloves, crushed
10 black peppercorns
2 bay leaves
a pinch of salt

1 Rinse the prepared octopus in plenty of water. Beat the tentacles lightly with a rolling pin or the flat side of a meat mallet.

2 Half-fill a large pan with water and add all the ingredients for the stock. Bring to the boil, lower the heat and simmer for 10 minutes.

3 Add the octopus and bring back to the boil. Lower the heat slightly to a slow boil, and cook for 1 hour.

4 If the octopus needs it, cook for longer, but check frequently because it will toughen if overcooked. Strain the stock into a bowl and reserve.

5 Whisk together the olive oil and vinegar in a bowl, then stir in the onion and parsley.

6 Cut the octopus into 2cm/¾in pieces and place in a dish. Pour the vinaigrette over and leave to stand for several hours before serving.

Nutritional information per portion: Energy 199kcal/834kJ; Protein 30g; Carbohydrate 0.5g, of which sugars 0.3g; Fat 8.6g, of which saturates 1.4g; Cholesterol 80mg; Calcium 60mg; Fibre 0.2g; Sodium 1mg.

Pasta and Rice

Pasta and fish complement each other beautifully, and many recipes are inspired by Mediterranean traditions. Fish and rice also have a natural affinity, and help to make a small amount of expensive fish go further. Whether you're making a luxurious creamy seafood lasagne or a tasty crab risotto, this chapter will give you plenty of new favourites to enjoy.

Creamy lemon and salmon pappardelle

This is a fantastic all-in-one supper dish that tastes great and is made in just a few minutes – ideal for when you have hungry people to feed but don't have much time.

SERVES 4

500g/1¼lb fresh tagliatelle or
    pappardelle
300ml/½ pint/1¼ cups single
    (light) cream
half a cucumber, halved and thinly sliced
grated rind and juice of 2 lemons
225g/8oz smoked salmon pieces
2.5ml/½ tsp grated nutmeg
60ml/4 tbsp chopped fresh dill, plus extra
    for garnishing
salt and ground black pepper
fresh Parmesan cheese shavings

1 Bring a large pan of lightly salted water to the boil and cook the pappardelle or tagliatelle for 3–5 minutes, or according to the instructions on the packet, until risen to the surface of the boiling water and just tender. Drain lightly.

2 Add the cream, sliced cucumber, lemon rind and juice to the pan and heat through gently until piping hot.

3 Return the pappardelle to the pan and stir into the creamy mixture.

4 Add the salmon pieces, nutmeg, parsley and plenty of ground black pepper to the sauce and stir to mix.

5 Divide the pasta among four warmed serving plates. Top with the fresh Parmesan shavings and chopped dill.

Nutritional information per portion: Energy 582kcal/2489kJ; Protein 28g; Carbohydrate 72g, of which sugars 4g; Fat 24g, of which saturates 10g; Cholesterol 69mg; Calcium 167mg; Fibre 0g; Sodium 83mg.

Smoked trout cannelloni

Cannelloni usually has a meat and tomato filling, or one based on spinach and ricotta cheese. Smoked trout makes a delicious alternative in this version.

SERVES 4–6

1 large onion, finely chopped
1 garlic clove, crushed
60ml/4 tbsp vegetable stock
2 x 400g/14oz cans chopped tomatoes
2.5ml/½ tsp dried mixed herbs
1 smoked trout, about 400g/14oz, or
**   225g/8oz fillets**
75g/3oz/½ cup frozen peas, thawed
75g/3oz/1½ cups fresh breadcrumbs
16 cannelloni tubes
25ml/1½ tbsp grated Parmesan cheese
salt and ground black pepper

FOR THE WHITE SAUCE
25g/1oz/2 tbsp butter
25g/1oz/¼ cup plain (all-purpose) flour
350ml/12fl oz/1½ cups skimmed milk
freshly grated nutmeg

1 Put the onion, garlic clove and stock in a large pan. Cover and simmer for 3 minutes. Remove the lid and cook until the stock has reduced entirely.

2 Stir in the tomatoes and dried herbs. Simmer uncovered for 10 minutes, or until the mixture is very thick.

3 Skin the trout and flake the flesh, discarding any bones. Put the fish in a bowl and add the tomato mixture, peas and breadcrumbs. Mix well, then season with salt and pepper.

4 Spoon the filling into the cannelloni tubes and arrange them in an ovenproof dish. Preheat the oven to 190°C/375°F/Gas 5.

5 Make the sauce. Put the butter, flour and milk into a pan and cook over medium heat, whisking constantly, until it thickens. Simmer for 2–3 minutes, stirring. Add salt, pepper and grated nutmeg.

6 Pour the sauce over the stuffed cannelloni and sprinkle with the Parmesan cheese. Bake for 30–45 minutes, until the top is golden.

Nutritional information per portion: Energy 410kcal/1735kJ; Protein 23.4g; Carbohydrate 62.3g, of which sugars 12g; Fat 9.3g, of which saturates 2.1g; Cholesterol 21mg; Calcium 186mg; Fibre 4.5g; Sodium 919mg.

Seafood lasagne

This dish can be adjusted to whatever fresh or smoked fish is available; you can use different quantities of each, as long as the overall weight is the same.

SERVES 8

350g/12oz monkfish
350g/12oz salmon fillet
350g/12oz smoked haddock
1 litre/1³⁄₄ pints/4 cups milk
500ml/17fl oz/2¹⁄₄ cups fish stock
2 bay leaves
1 small onion, halved
75g/3oz/6 tbsp butter
45ml/3 tbsp plain (all-purpose) flour
150g/5oz/2 cups mushrooms, sliced
225–300g/8–11oz fresh lasagne
60ml/4 tbsp freshly grated Parmesan cheese
salt, ground black pepper, grated nutmeg
   and paprika

FOR THE TOMATO SAUCE

30ml/2 tbsp olive oil
1 red onion, finely chopped
1 garlic clove, finely chopped
400g/14oz can chopped tomatoes
15ml/1 tbsp tomato purée (paste)

1 For the tomato sauce, fry the onion and garlic for 5 minutes. Stir in the tomatoes and tomato purée, season, and simmer for 20–30 minutes, stirring occasionally.

2 Put all the fish in a pan with the milk, stock, bay leaves or saffron and onion. Poach for 5 minutes. When cool, strain the liquid and reserve it. Remove skin and bones, then flake the fish.

3 Preheat the oven to 180°C/350°F/ Gas 4. Melt the butter in a pan and stir in the flour. Cook for 2 minutes, stirring. Add the poaching liquid and bring to the boil, stirring.

4 Add the mushrooms to the sauce. Cook for 2 minutes. Season with salt, pepper and nutmeg.

5 Grease a shallow ovenproof dish. Spread a thin layer of mushroom sauce in the dish. Stir the fish into the remaining sauce in the pan. Add a layer of lasagne to the dish, then a layer of fish and sauce, then a layer of lasagne, then spread over all the tomato sauce. Add a layer of lasagne and finish with a layer of fish. Sprinkle over the cheese.

6 Bake for 30–45 minutes, until golden. Leave for 10 minutes, then sprinkle with paprika and serve.

Nutritional information per portion: Energy 411kcal/1724kJ; Protein 32.2g; Carbohydrate 29.8g, of which sugars 3.6g; Fat 18.9g, of which saturates 7.8g; Cholesterol 71mg; Calcium 143mg; Fibre 1.9g; Sodium 525mg.

Tagliatelle with cuttlefish and shrimp

This is a very simple combination of tastes and textures, put together to create a sumptuous pasta dish inspired by traditional seafood recipes from the Italian coastal region.

SERVES 4

120ml/4fl oz/½ cup olive oil

1 garlic clove

a pinch of crushed chilli flakes

450g/1lb cuttlefish, cleaned and cut into small cubes

275g/10oz raw shrimp tails or prawns (shrimp), peeled and chopped

175ml/6fl oz/¾ cup dry white wine

3 ripe tomatoes, peeled, seeded and diced

350g/12oz fresh tagliatelle

sea salt

a handful of fresh flat leaf parsley, leaves chopped, to garnish

1 Put the olive oil, garlic clove and chilli flakes into a pan and fry gently until the garlic is golden brown.

2 Add the cuttlefish and shrimp tails or prawns, and stir together until the seafood is coated with the oil.

3 Add the white wine to the pan, bring to the boil and simmer gently for 1–2 minutes.

4 Add the diced tomatoes and stir well. Simmer for 5 minutes and season with salt.

5 Meanwhile, cook the tagliatelle in a large pan of salted boiling water, until the pasta is just cooked. Drain the pasta and return it to the pan. Add the sauce and mix together gently. Serve immediately, sprinkled with the fresh parsley.

Nutritional information per portion: Energy 630kcal/2654kJ; Protein 41.3g; Carbohydrate 67.4g, of which sugars 5.5g; Fat 20.5g, of which saturates 3g; Cholesterol 258mg; Calcium 152mg; Fibre 3.3g; Sodium 558mg.

Baked trout with rice, tomatoes and nuts

Trout is very popular in Spain, particularly in the north, where it is fished in many rivers. Here it is baked in foil with a rice stuffing in which sun-dried tomatoes have been used in place of chillies.

SERVES 4

2 fresh trout, about 500g/1¼lb each, deboned but left whole

75g/3oz/¾ cup mixed unsalted almonds, pine nuts or hazelnuts

25ml/1½ tbsp olive oil, plus extra for drizzling

1 small onion, finely chopped

10ml/2 tsp grated fresh root ginger

175g/6oz/1½ cups cooked white long grain rice

4 tomatoes, peeled and very chopped

4 sun-dried tomatoes in oil, drained and chopped

30ml/2 tbsp chopped fresh tarragon

2 fresh tarragon sprigs

salt and ground black pepper

dressed green salad leaves, to serve

1 Preheat the oven to 190°C/375°F/Gas 5. Remove any tiny bones remaining in the trout cavities, using a pair of tweezers.

2 Spread out the nuts in a baking tray and bake for 3–4 minutes until golden brown, shaking the tray occasionally. Chop the nuts roughly.

3 Heat the olive oil in a frying pan and fry the onion for 3–4 minutes until soft. Stir in the ginger, cook for 1 minute, then transfer to a bowl.

4 Stir the rice, tomatoes, sun-dried tomatoes, toasted nuts and tarragon into the onion mixture. Season well.

5 Place each trout on a large piece of oiled foil and spoon the stuffing into the cavities. Add a sprig of tarragon and a drizzle of olive oil.

6 Fold the foil over to enclose each trout, and put the parcels in a roasting pan. Bake for about 20 minutes. Cut the fish into thick slices. Serve with the salad leaves.

Nutritional information per portion: Energy 458kcal/1920kJ; Protein 45.1g; Carbohydrate 19.4g, of which sugars 5g; Fat 22.8g, of which saturates 3.4g; Cholesterol 160mg; Calcium 146mg; Fibre 3.2g; Sodium 161mg

North African fish with pumpkin rice

The slightly sweet pumpkin, in this Moroccan recipe, is a good partner for the mildly spicy fish. If sea bass isn't available, use cod or haddock fillet instead.

SERVES 4

450g/1lb sea bass fillet, cut into chunks
30ml/2 tbsp plain (all purpose) flour
5ml/1 tsp ground coriander
1.5–2.5ml/¼–½ tsp ground turmeric
1 wedge of pumpkin, about 500g/1¼lb,
    deseeded and cut into bitesize chunks
30–45ml/2–3 tbsp olive oil
6 spring onions (scallions), sliced
1 garlic clove, finely chopped
275g/10oz/1½ cups basmati rice, soaked
550ml/18fl oz/2½ cups fish stock
salt and ground black pepper
lemon wedges, to serve

FOR THE SPICE MIXTURE

45ml/3 tbsp chopped coriander (cilantro)
10ml/2 tsp finely chopped fresh root ginger
½–1 red chilli, seeded and finely chopped
45ml/3 tbsp lime or lemon juice

1 Mix the flour, ground coriander, turmeric and salt and pepper in a plastic bag, add the fish and shake until the fish is evenly coated. Set aside. Make the spice mixture by mixing all the ingredients in a bowl.

2 Heat 15ml/1 tbsp oil in a casserole and stir-fry the spring onions and garlic for a few minutes. Add the pumpkin and cook over a low heat, stirring frequently, for 4–5 minutes.

3 Drain the rice, add it to the mixture and toss over a brisk heat for 2 minutes. Stir in the stock.

4 Bring to the boil, lower the heat, cover and cook for 12–15 minutes until the pumpkin is tender, and the rice has absorbed all the stock.

5 About 4 minutes before the rice is ready, heat the remaining oil in a frying pan and fry the spiced fish for about 3 minutes, turning, until crisp and golden.

6 Stir the spice mixture into the rice and transfer to a serving dish. Lay the fried fish pieces on top. Serve immediately, with lemon wedges to squeeze over the fish.

Nutritional information per portion: Energy 499kcal/2104kJ; Protein 29g; Carbohydrate 70g, of which sugars 3g; Fat 14g, of which saturates 2g; Cholesterol 90mg; Calcium 210mg; Fibre 2g; Sodium 379mg.

Paella Valenciana

*Valencia's paella has become a national celebration dish throughout Spain.
It is often taken into the countryside or to the beach for day-long picnics, when it
is often cooked on a wood fire or barbeque and eaten straight from the pan.*

SERVES 6–8

90ml/6 tbsp white wine

450g/1lb fresh mussels, scrubbed

115g/4oz/scant 1 cup fresh shelled broad
   (fava) beans

150g/5oz green beans, cut into pieces

90ml/6 tbsp olive oil

6 chicken breast fillets, cut into four

150g/5oz pork fillet, cubed

6–8 large raw prawn (shrimp) tails

2 onions, chopped

2–3 garlic cloves, finely chopped

1 red (bell) pepper, seeded and sliced

2 tomatoes, peeled, seeded and chopped

60ml/4 tbsp chopped fresh parsley

900ml/1½ pints/3¾ cups chicken
   stock

a pinch of saffron threads, soaked in
   30ml/2 tbsp water

350g/12oz/1¾ cups paella rice, washed
   and drained

225g/8oz cooking chorizo, thickly sliced

115g/4oz/1 cup peas

6–8 stuffed green olives, sliced

salt, paprika and black pepper

1 Heat the wine and add the mussels, cover and steam until open. Reserve the liquid and mussels separately, discarding any that do not open. Briefly cook the broad beans and green beans, then drain. Skin the broad beans.

2 Heat 45ml/3 tbsp oil in a large paella pan. Season the chicken with salt and paprika, and brown on all sides. Set aside. Season the pork with salt and paprika. Add 15ml/1 tbsp oil and fry the pork until browned. Set aside with the chicken. Fry the prawns in the same pan and reserve.

3 Heat the remaining oil and fry the onions, garlic and red pepper for 5–7 minutes, then stir in the tomatoes and parsley and cook until thick. Add the chicken stock, the mussel stock and the saffron liquid to the vegetables. Season and, when bubbling, add the rice. Stir, then add the chicken, pork, beans, chorizo and peas.

4 Cook for 10–15 minutes until the rice is tender. Put the prawns, mussels and olives on top. Stand for 10 minutes, covered, until all the liquid is completely absorbed. Serve from the pan.

Nutritional information per portion: Energy 712kcal/2978kJ; Protein 69.9g; Carbohydrate 48g, of which sugars 5.8g; Fat 26.1g, of which saturates 6.4g; Cholesterol 208mg; Calcium 98mg; Fibre 3.6g; Sodium 468mg.

Fried chilli fish with spicy rice

Cooking rice in a rich fish stock until it is all absorbed gives it a splendid flavour and a lovely sticky finish. This is a recipe in which you can use whatever white fish is available.

SERVES 6

45ml/3 tbsp olive oil

6 garlic cloves, smashed

1 dried chilli, seeded and chopped

250g/9oz ripe tomatoes, peeled, seeded and chopped

pinch of saffron threads

1.6kg/3½lb mixed fish fillets such as snapper, mullet, or bass

1 litre/1¾ pints/4 cups fish stock

30ml/2 tbsp dry white wine

1 tomato, finely diced

30ml/2 tbsp chopped fresh parsley

400g/14oz/2 cups paella rice

115g/4oz tiny unshelled shrimps

salt and ground black pepper

FOR THE AIOLI

4 garlic cloves, finely chopped

2.5ml/½ tsp salt

5ml/1 tsp lemon juice

2 egg yolks

250ml/8fl oz/1 cup olive oil

1 To make the aioli, put the chopped garlic in a large mortar (or blender) with the salt and lemon juice and pound to a purée. Add the egg yolks and mix. Gradually work in the oil to make a thick, mayonnaise-like sauce.

2 Now prepare the fish. put 15ml/1 tbsp of the olive oil in a small pan and add the smashed garlic cloves and dried chilli. Fry for a few minutes then add the chopped tomato and saffron. Cook for a few minutes, then transfer to a processor and blend until smooth.

3 Heat the remaining 30ml/2 tbsp oil in a large pan or a wide flameproof casserole, and fry the fish pieces until they begin to stiffen. Add the fish stock and the tomato sauce to the pan and cook gently for 3–4 minutes.

4 Transfer the fish to a serving dish. Season, then sprinkle with the wine, diced tomato and parsley. Cover with foil and keep warm.

5 Add the rice to the stock, stir, season and bring to a simmer. Cook for 18–20 minutes. Before all the liquid is absorbed, stir in the shrimps. When the rice is tender, cover and turn off the heat. Leave to stand until all the liquid is absorbed: about 5 minutes. Serve with the fish fillets and aioli.

Nutritional information per portion: Energy 809kcal/3367kJ; Protein 56.9g; Carbohydrate 55.6g, of which sugars 1.9g; Fat 39g, of which saturates 5.8g; Cholesterol 198mg; Calcium 71mg; Fibre 0.7g; Sodium 412mg.

Stuffed squid

This is a wonderful way to cook fresh squid, as it helps to keep the flesh tender. Make sure you buy squid that hasn't been previously frozen, as it will not give such a good result.

SERVES 4

1kg/2¼lb squid, preferably about
    10cm/4in long, rinsed under cold
    running water
150ml/¼ pint/⅔ cup olive oil
4 onions, chopped
2 garlic cloves, chopped
100g/3¾oz cured ham, chopped
150g/5oz sausage or bacon, chopped
4 large ripe tomatoes, peeled and
    chopped
100g/3¾oz/generous ½ cup cooked
    rice
1 bay leaf
1 bunch of parsley, chopped
salt
sautéed potatoes and tomato and parsley
    salad, to serve

1 Pull the squid heads away from the body to remove the entrails. Cut off the tentacles, squeeze out and discard the 'beak'. Pull out and discard the transparent 'quill' from the body sac and clean any remaining membrane. Rinse the body sac and peel off the skin. Chop up the tentacles.

2 Heat a third of the oil in a pan. Add half the onions and half the garlic. Cook, stirring, for 5 minutes. Add the chopped tentacles, ham and sausage or bacon, and cook for a few minutes more. Stir in a quarter of the tomatoes and all the rice. Mix and remove the pan from the heat.

3 Spoon the filling into the body sacs of the squid, filling them just over half full. Secure the openings with wooden cocktail sticks (toothpicks).

4 Heat the remaining oil in a large pan. Add the remaining onions and garlic and cook over a low heat, stirring occasionally, for 5 minutes, until softened. Add the bay leaf and remaining tomatoes and about 150ml/¼ pint/⅔ cup water. Stir in the parsley and add the squid.

5 Season with salt and simmer gently for about 20 minutes, until tender. Serve with cooked potatoes.

Nutritional information per portion: Energy 418kcal/1758kJ; Protein 37.7g; Carbohydrate 20.7g, of which sugars 7.4g; Fat 21.2g, of which saturates 5.9g; Cholesterol 456mg; Calcium 245mg; Fibre 2.6g; Sodium 508mg.

Truffle and lobster risotto

To enhance the qualities of a precious truffle, it is partnered here with lobster and served in a silky risotto. Adding truffle shavings and oil toward the end of cooking preserves the unique flavour.

SERVES 4

50g/2oz/4 tbsp unsalted butter
1 medium onion, chopped
350g/12oz/1³/₄ cups risotto rice,
 preferably Carnaroli
a fresh sprig of thyme
150ml/¹/₄ pint/²/₃ cup dry white wine
1.2 litres/2 pints/5 cups simmering
 chicken stock
1 freshly cooked lobster, meat removed
45ml/3 tbsp chopped mixed fresh parsley
 and chervil
3–4 drops truffle oil
2 hard-boiled eggs
1 fresh black or white truffle
salt and freshly ground black pepper

1 Melt the butter, add the onion and fry until soft. Add the rice and stir to coat. Add the thyme, then the wine, and cook until it has been absorbed. Add the chicken stock a little at a time, stirring. Let each ladleful be absorbed before adding the next.

2 Cut half the lobster meat into large chunks, then roughly chop the remainder. Stir the chopped lobster meat, half the chopped herbs and the truffle oil into the risotto.

3 Remove the risotto from the heat, cover and allow to stand for 5 minutes. Divide among four warmed plates and place the reserved lobster chunks on top in the centre of the risotto. Cut the hard-boiled eggs into wedges and arrange them around the lobster.

5 Finally, shave a little fresh truffle over each portion and sprinkle with the remaining chopped fresh parsley and chervil. Serve immediately.

Nutritional information per portion: Energy 520kcal/2172kJ; Protein 19.9g; Carbohydrate 71.3g, of which sugars 1.2g; Fat 14.3g, of which saturates 7.4g; Cholesterol 172mg; Calcium 68mg; Fibre 0.2g; Sodium 263mg.

Crab risotto

This is a fresh-flavoured risotto which makes a wonderful main course or appetizer. You will need two crabs for this recipe, and it is a good dish to make when crabs are cheap and plentiful.

SERVES 3–4

2 large cooked crabs, meat removed from
    the body cavities, claws and legs using
    a small hammer or crab crackers and a
    pick or skewer
15ml/1 tbsp olive oil
25g/1oz/2 tbsp butter
2 shallots, finely chopped
275g/10oz/1½ cups risotto rice,
    preferably Carnaroli
75ml/5 tbsp Marsala or brandy
1 litre/1¾ pints/4 cups simmering
    fish stock
5ml/1 tsp chopped fresh tarragon
5ml/1 tsp chopped fresh parsley
60ml/4 tbsp double (heavy) cream
salt and freshly ground black pepper

1 Using a pick or a skewer, remove the white meat from the body cavities and place on the plate with the meat from the claws and legs, reserving some for garnish. Scoop out the brown meat from the shell and set aside with the white meat.

2 Heat the oil and butter in a pan and fry the shallots until soft but not browned. Add the rice. Cook for a few minutes, then add the Marsala or brandy, bring to the boil, and cook, stirring, until it has evaporated. Add a ladleful of hot stock and cook, stirring, until absorbed.

3 Continue until about two-thirds of the stock has been added, then stir all of the brown crab meat, and most of the white, reserving some with crab meat. Stir in the herbs. Continue to cook the risotto, adding the remaining stock.

4 When the rice is almost cooked but still has a slight 'bite', remove it from the heat, add the cream and season.

5 Cover and leave to stand for 3 minutes to finish cooking. Serve, garnished with the reserved white crab meat.

Nutritional information per portion: Energy 496kcal/2060kJ; Protein 14.1g; Carbohydrate 56.4g, of which sugars 1.1g; Fat 18.7g, of which saturates 8.9g; Cholesterol 65mg; Calcium 25mg; Fibre 0.2g; Sodium 229mg.

Braised octopus with rice

While it has a delicate flavour, octopus has a reputation for being chewy. Its texture largely depends on its origin and quality, but also on how it is cooked.

SERVES 4

1 octopus, about 1.6kg/3½ lb, cleaned, trimmed and beak removed; cut the tentacles off and beat the body with a rolling pin to tenderize
150ml/¼ pint/⅔ cup olive oil
2 onions, chopped
300g/11oz/generous 1½ cups long grain rice
1 bay leaf

FOR THE STOCK

2 onions, quartered
1 leek, chopped
3 garlic cloves, crushed
10 black peppercorns
2 bay leaves
a pinch of salt

1 Half-fill a large pan with water and add all the ingredients for the stock. Bring to the boil, lower the heat and simmer for 10 minutes.

2 Add the octopus to the stock and bring back to the boil. Lower the heat slightly to simmer, and cook for 1 hour. Check with a fork to see if the octopus is tender. If not, cook for a little longer but check frequently so it does not overcook.

3 Strain the stock into a bowl. Dice the octopus body and cut the tentacles into lengths, keeping the two parts separate.

4 Preheat the oven to 160°C/325°F/Gas 3. Heat 50ml/2fl oz/¼ cup of the olive oil in a flameproof casserole. Add the onions and cook over a low heat for 10 minutes.

5 Add the rice, the octopus body, the bay leaf and 600ml/1 pint/2½ cups of the reserved stock to the casserole. Transfer to the oven and braise for 30 minutes.

6 Meanwhile, place the tentacles in an ovenproof dish, pour the remaining olive oil over them and heat through in the oven. Combine with the rice mixture before serving.

Nutritional information per portion: Energy 871kcal/3646kJ; Protein 78.8g; Carbohydrate 69.7g, of which sugars 7g; Fat 30.9g, of which saturates 4.8g; Cholesterol 192mg; Calcium 178mg; Fibre 1.8g; Sodium 95mg.

Poached, Grilled and Steamed

The tender flesh of a delicate white fish lends itself well to gentle poaching and steaming, keeping it moist and retaining flavour. Grilling is ideal, however, for the more robust types of oily fish and shellfish, adding another level of taste and texture, and cooking quickly under high temperatures helps to keep the flavour locked in.

Haddock with dill sauce

Dill is a classic herb to accompany fish, and here it is used to lift a simple cream sauce partnered with moist fillets of poached haddock. Serve this on its own, or with seasonal vegetables.

SERVES 4

50g/2oz/¼ cup butter
4 haddock fillets, about 185g/6½ oz each
200ml/7fl oz/scant 1 cup milk
200ml/7fl oz/scant 1 cup fish stock
3–4 bay leaves
75ml/5 tbsp plain (all-purpose) flour
150ml/¼ pint/²/₃ cup double (heavy) cream
1 egg yolk
30ml–45ml/2–3 tbsp chopped fresh dill
salt and ground black pepper, to taste
dill fronds and slices of lemon, to garnish (optional)

1 Melt 25g/1oz/2 tbsp butter in a frying pan, then add the haddock fillets, milk, fish stock, bay leaves, and salt and black pepper to taste.

2 Bring to a simmer, then poach the fish gently over a low heat for 10–15 minutes until tender.

3 Meanwhile, melt the remaining butter in a small pan, add the flour and cook, stirring, for 2 minutes. Remove the pan from the heat and slowly add the double cream, whisking constantly to make a smooth sauce.

4 Stir the egg yolk in to the sauce, together with the chopped fresh dill, then return to the heat and simmer for 4 minutes, or until the sauce has thickened. Do not allow the sauce to boil. Season to taste with salt and black pepper.

5 Using a slotted spoon, remove the haddock fillets to a serving dish or four warmed serving plates, and pour over the hot sauce.

6 Garnish the fish with dill fronds and slices of lemon, if you like, and serve immediately.

Nutritional information per portion: Energy 503kcal/2097kJ; Protein 36.6g; Carbohydrate 15.5g, of which sugars 1.2g; Fat 33.2g, of which saturates 19.6g; Cholesterol 191mg; Calcium 92mg; Fibre 1g; Sodium 207mg.

Smoked haddock with spinach and poached egg

This makes a perfect breakfast treat. There is something about the combination of eggs, spinach and smoked fish that really lifts your spirits up in the morning.

SERVES 4

4 undyed smoked haddock fillets
milk, for poaching
75ml/2½ fl oz/⅓ cup double
  (heavy) cream
25g/1oz/2 tbsp butter
250g/9oz fresh spinach, tough
  stalks removed
white wine vinegar
4 eggs
salt and ground black pepper

1 Over a low heat, poach the haddock fillets in just enough milk to come halfway up the fish, for about 5 minutes. When cooked remove the fish and keep warm.

2 Increase the heat under the milk reduce by about half, stirring. Add the cream and heat until it bubbles up. Season with salt and ground black pepper. The sauce should be thickened but should pour easily.

3 Heat the butter in a frying pan then add the spinach, stirring briskly for a few minutes until just wilted.

4 To poach the eggs, bring a large pan of water to a simmer and add a few drops of vinegar.

5 Gently crack two eggs into the water and cook for 3 minutes. Remove with a slotted spoon and rest on kitchen paper to remove any water. Cook the other two in the same way.

6 Place the spinach over the haddock fillets on four warmed serving plates, and put a poached egg on top. Pour over the cream sauce and serve immediately.

Nutritional information per portion: Energy 350kcal/1455kJ; Protein 27.5g; Carbohydrate 1.5g, of which sugars 1.4g; Fat 26.3g, of which saturates 14g; Cholesterol 277mg; Calcium 170mg; Fibre 1.3g; Sodium 969mg.

White fish dumplings

These delicate fish dumplings are served on a bed of summer vegetables and accompanied by a creamy white wine sauce. Any white fish fillets can be used in this recipe.

SERVES 4

500g/1¼lb whole white fish, such as carp, filleted, heads, tails and bone retained

2 eggs, separated

5ml/1 tsp salt

2.5ml/½ tsp ground white pepper

200ml/7fl oz/scant 1 cup double (heavy) cream

25ml/1½ tbsp vegetable oil

1 onion, chopped

1 small celery stick, chopped

300ml/½ pint/1¼ cups white wine

50g/2oz/¼ cup unsalted butter

30ml/2 tbsp plain (all-purpose) flour

15ml/1 tbsp chopped fresh dill

salt, cayenne pepper and ground black pepper

cooked early summer vegetables, such as peas, baby carrots and turnips, asparagus and spinach, to serve

1 Cut the fish fillets into small dice, put in the bowl of a food processor and blend until finely chopped, slowly adding the egg whites, salt and pepper while blending. Put the fish paste in a bowl and place in the freezer for 20 minutes, until very cold but not frozen. Beat in half the cream and cayenne pepper, then set aside in the refrigerator.

2 Heat the oil in a pan, add the onion and celery and fry until softened. Add the fish heads, bones and tails. Pour in half of the wine, and enough water to just cover. Bring to the boil, reduce the heat and simmer for 20 minutes. Strain the stock into a clean pan. You should have about 400ml/14fl oz/ 1²/₃ cups fish stock.

3 Simmer the stock. Use two tablespoons to shape the fish mixture into balls and drop into the stock in two or three batches. Cook for 5 minutes, turning them gently. Transfer to an ovenproof dish and keep warm in a cool oven.

4 Melt the butter in a pan, stir in the flour to make a roux, then stir in a ladleful of the fish stock. Slowly bring to the boil, stirring all the time, until the sauce thickens to a smooth, velvety texture.

5 Stir the remaining wine and cream into the sauce, return to the boil then remove from the heat. Whisk in the egg yolks and dill, pour the sauce over the dumplings and serve over the vegetables.

Nutritional information per portion: Energy 600kcal/2484kJ; Protein 27.7g; Carbohydrate 6.5g, of which sugars 2.4g; Fat 46.4g, of which saturates 24.8g; Cholesterol 248mg; Calcium 73mg; Fibre 0.5g; Sodium 205mg.

Poached fish in spicy tomato sauce

A selection of white fish fillets are used in this Middle-Eastern dish – cod, haddock, hake or halibut all work well. Serve the fish with flat breads, such as pitta, and a spicy tomato relish.

SERVES 8

600ml/1 pint/2½ cups fresh tomato sauce

2.5–5ml/½–1 tsp harissa

60ml/4 tbsp chopped fresh coriander (cilantro) leaves

1.5kg/3¼lb mixed white fish fillets, cut into chunks

1 Heat the tomato sauce with the harissa and coriander in a large pan. Add seasoning to taste and bring to the boil.

2 Remove the pan from the heat and add the fish to the hot sauce. Return to the heat and bring the sauce back to the boil.

3 Reduce the heat and simmer very gently for about 5 minutes, or until the fish is tender.

4 Test the fish with a fork: if the flesh flakes easily, then it is cooked.

5 Taste the sauce and adjust the seasoning, adding more harissa if necessary. Serve hot or warm.

COOK'S TIP

Harissa, a hot chilli sauce spiced with cumin, garlic and coriander, is a standard ingredient in many North African dishes. Start by adding a small amount and then add more if you wish, after tasting.

Nutritional information per portion: Energy 194kcal/823kJ; Protein 37g; Carbohydrate 5g, of which sugars 4g; Fat 3g, of which saturates 0g; Cholesterol 68mg; Calcium 45mg; Fibre 1g; Sodium 450mg.

Fish poached in vinegar and ginger

This method of cooking in vinegar and sugar dates back to Roman times. Although simple, it is a well-regarded method, and firm-fleshed fish turns out particularly well when prepared this way.

SERVES 4

30ml/2 tbsp garlic purée (paste)

30ml/2 tbsp grated ginger

5ml/1 tsp black peppercorns, crushed

300ml/½ pint/1¼ cups water

105ml/7 tbsp vinegar

2 whole fish (600g/1lb 6oz total weight) such as mullet, cod or snapper

15ml/1 tbsp Thai fish sauce

15ml/1 tbsp vegetable oil

fresh coriander (cilantro) leaves and a few chilli strips, to garnish

1 Blend the garlic purée, ginger, crushed peppercorns, water and vinegar in a non-metallic bowl. Place in a flameproof dish.

2 Clean and gut the fish, trimming off any protruding fins and tail with scissors, and add to the dish.

3 Bring to the boil, then simmer for 5 minutes, covered. Turn the fish gently, and with a ladle add the Thai fish sauce and oil. Simmer for another 3 minutes. Serve the fish hot, with the cooking liquid poured over it, garnished with coriander leaves and chilli strips.

Nutritional information per portion: Energy 157kcal/658kJ; Protein 28g; Carbohydrate 1.5g, of which sugars 0.4g; Fat 4.3g, of which saturates 0.9g; Cholesterol 78mg; Calcium 40mg; Fibre 0.3g; Sodium 411mg.

Poached turbot with saffron sauce

Turbot is a treat by any standards and this is a rich, elegant dish, most suitable for entertaining. Serve buttered boiled new potatoes, and green beans or peas with the turbot.

SERVES 4

a pinch of saffron threads
50ml/2fl oz/¼ cup single (light) cream
1 shallot, finely chopped
175g/6oz/¾ cup cold unsalted butter,
   cut into small cubes
175ml/6fl oz/¾ cup dry sherry
475ml/16fl oz/2 cups fish stock
4 medium turbot fillets, about
   150–175g/5–6oz each, skinned
flat leaf parsley leaves, to garnish

1 Put the saffron threads into the single cream and allow them to infuse (steep) for 10 minutes. Cook the shallot very gently in a large heavy-based frying pan with 15g/ ½oz/1 tbsp of the butter until soft.

2 Put the cooked shallot, with the dry sherry and fish stock, into a fish kettle or other large, heavy pan.

3 Lay the turbot fillets in the pan and bring gently to the boil. Reduce the heat and simmer for about 5 minutes, depending on the thickness of the fish.

4 When cooked, remove the fillets from the poaching liquid with a slotted fish slice or metal spatula and keep warm.

5 Bring the poaching liquor to the boil and boil fast to reduce it to 60ml/4 tbsp. Add the cream and saffron and bring back to the boil. Remove from the heat, and add the butter, whisking constantly until a smooth sauce has formed.

6 Pour the sauce on to warmed serving plates, lay the turbot on top and sprinkle with parsley leaves.

Nutritional information per portion: Energy 544Kcal/2256kJ; Protein 27.4g; Carbohydrate 1.4g, of which sugars 1.4g; Fat 42.4g, of which saturates 25.4g; Cholesterol 100mg; Calcium 97mg; Fibre 0.1g; Sodium 376mg.

Marinated steamed sea bass

This is a South American version of an ancient technique for cooking fish. The fish is steamed with a little vinegar or chicha, which is a drink made from fermented corn.

SERVES 2

1 sea bass, weighing about 500g/1¼lb, scaled and cleaned
2.5ml/½ tsp ground black pepper
2.5ml/½ tsp ground cumin
45ml/3 tbsp red wine vinegar
75ml/5 tbsp vegetable oil
1 large red onion, chopped
1 small tomato, chopped
1 small piece of red (bell) pepper, diced
1 chilli, seeded and finely chopped
15ml/1 tbsp grated garlic
10ml/2 tsp paprika
salt
boiled cassava or potato, to serve

1 Season the sea bass with pepper, cumin and salt. Pour the vinegar over it and leave to marinate for 15 minutes.

2 Heat the oil in a large frying pan and fry the onion for 5 minutes over medium heat. When it starts to brown, add the chopped tomato, diced pepper, chopped chilli, garlic and paprika, and cook for a further 5 minutes.

3 Lay the fish in the pan and pour in its seasonings and vinegar.

4 Cover the pan and leave the fish to steam for 15 minutes.

5 Using a fork, carefully check that the fish is cooked: if the flesh flakes easily, remove from the heat. Serve the fish accompanied by the tomato mixture, and boiled cassava, if using, or boiled potatoes.

COOK'S TIP

Cassava is a tropical vegetable with starchy roots that is rather like a yam. After peeling, the creamy white flesh is cooked and eaten instead of potatoes.

Nutritional information per portion: Energy 592kcal/2471kJ; Protein 50.6g; Carbohydrate 27.8g, of which sugars 21.2g; Fat 31.8g, of which saturates 4g; Cholesterol 120mg; Calcium 77mg; Fibre 5.7g; Sodium 750mg.

Sole with vodka sauce and caviar

Caviar is as much of an expensive delicacy as it has ever been, but for a special occasion the luxurious effect and stylish elegance you'll achieve for your guests is well worth it.

SERVES 4

500–600g/1lb 4oz–1lb 6oz sole, flounder
    or plaice fillets
200ml/7fl oz/scant 1 cup fish stock
60ml/4 tbsp caviar
salt
4 lemon wedges and fresh dill,
    to garnish
hot boiled potatoes, to serve

FOR THE VODKA SAUCE

25–40g/1–1¹/₂oz/2–3 tbsp butter
5–6 shallots, finely diced
5ml/1 tsp plain white (all-purpose) flour
200ml/7fl oz/scant 1 cup double (heavy) cream
200ml/7fl oz/scant 1 cup fish stock
100ml/3¹/₂fl oz/scant ¹/₂ cup dry white wine
30ml/2 tbsp vodka
salt and ground black pepper

1 Season the fish fillets with salt. Roll up and secure each fillet with a cocktail stick (toothpick).

2 Heat the stock in a small pan. Place the fish rolls in the pan, cover and simmer for 5–8 minutes, until the fish is tender. Remove from the pan and keep warm.

3 Meanwhile, make the sauce. Melt the butter in a pan, add the shallots and fry gently for 3–5 minutes, until softened but not browned. Add the flour and stir until well mixed.

4 Gradually add the cream and stock until smooth. Slowly bring to the boil, stirring, until the sauce bubbles. Reduce the heat and simmer for 3–5 minutes, until the sauce thickens. Remove the shallots with a slotted spoon. Add the wine and vodka and bring to the boil. Season with salt and pepper to taste.

5 Pour the sauce over the base of four warmed plates. Place the fish rolls on top and add a spoonful of caviar to each. Garnish with lemon and dill, and serve with hot boiled potatoes.

Nutritional information per portion: Energy 470kcal/1952kJ; Protein 27.9g; Carbohydrate 3.2g, of which sugars 1.9g; Fat 35g, of which saturates 20.4g; Cholesterol 188mg; Calcium 103mg; Fibre 0.3g; Sodium 548mg.

Paper-wrapped and steamed red snapper

Traditionally, this elegant dish from Japan featured a red snapper wrapped in layered hand-made paper, then soaked in sake and tied with ribbons.

SERVES 4

4 small red snapper fillets, no greater than 18 x 6cm/7 x 2½ in, or whole snapper, 20cm/8in long, gutted but head, tail and fins intact

8 asparagus spears, hard ends discarded

4 spring onions (scallions)

60ml/4 tbsp sake

grated rind of ½ lime

½ lime, thinly sliced

5ml/1 tsp soy sauce, for serving

salt

1 Sprinkle the fish fillets with salt and chill for 20 minutes. Preheat the oven to 180°C/350°F/ Gas 4.

2 Cut 2.5cm/1in from the tips of the asparagus. Slice the asparagus stems and spring onions diagonally into thin ovals. Blanch the tips for 1 minute and drain. Set aside.

3 To make the parcels, lay four squares of baking parchment or foil measuring 45 x 45cm/18 x 18in on a work surface. Place the asparagus and the spring onions inside. Sprinkle with salt and place the fish on top. Add more salt and some sake, then the lime rind.

4 Bring the edges of the foil or paper over to enclose the fish, and seal well by folding the edges. Leave some air space in the parcels – they should not be wrapped tightly.

5 Pour hot water into a roasting pan fitted with a wire rack to 1cm/½in below the rack. Place the parcels on the rack. Cook in the centre of the oven for 15–20 minutes.

6 Transfer the parcels on to individual plates, and top each with a thin slice of lime and two asparagus tips. Serve, asking the guests to open their own parcels, with a little soy sauce.

Nutritional information per portion: Energy 110kcal/465kJ; Protein 20.6g; Carbohydrate 1g, of which sugars 0.9g; Fat 1.5g, of which saturates 0.3g; Cholesterol 37mg; Calcium 51mg; Fibre 0.6g; Sodium 79mg.

Poached salmon steaks with parsley butter sauce

For sheer simplicity, this dish takes a lot of beating. The deliciously rich parsley butter sauce is a traditional Norwegian accompaniment to many fish dishes.

SERVES 4

4 salmon steaks, each about 175g/6oz
1 litre/1³/₄ pints/4 cups water
45ml/3 tbsp salt
5ml/1 tsp whole peppercorns
1 lemon slice
1 onion slice
**cucumber salad, dressed with vinegar and
    chopped dill, to serve**

**FOR THE PARSLEY BUTTER
SAUCE**
**100ml/3¹/₂ fl oz/scant ¹/₂ cup double
    (heavy) cream**
**225g/8oz/1 cup chilled unsalted butter,
    cut into small cubes**
**30–45ml/2–3 tbsp chopped fresh parsley
    or chives**

1 Put the fish steaks, in a single layer, in a pan and add the water to cover. Add the salt, peppercorns, lemon and onion slice.

2 Bring to the boil, then lower the heat to below simmering point. (The water just should throw up the occasional bubble.) Poach for 6–8 minutes, until the flesh easily loosens from the backbone.

3 To make the sauce, pour the cream into a pan and slowly bring to the boil.

4 Lower the heat and gradually add the butter, in small pieces, whisking all the time. Add another piece only when the one before is incorporated. Do not allow the sauce to boil or it will separate.

5 If you wish, the sauce can be kept warm in a bowl standing over a pan of gently simmering water.

6 Just before serving, add the parsley or chives to the sauce. Serve the fish and the sauce with a cucumber salad.

Nutritional information per portion: Energy 771kcal/3184kJ; Protein 26.3g; Carbohydrate 1.1g, of which sugars 1g; Fat 73.6g, of which saturates 40g; Cholesterol 217mg; Calcium 71mg; Fibre 0.6g; Sodium 406mg.

Lobster and crab steamed in beer

Cooking lobster may seem daunting if you haven't done it before, but actually this Thai recipe is a very easy dish to achieve. Depending on the size and availability of the lobsters and crabs, you can easily adapt the quantities for as many or few people as you like.

SERVES 4

4 uncooked lobsters, about 450g/1lb each
4–8 uncooked crabs, about 225g/8oz each
about 600ml/1 pint/2½ cups beer
4 spring onions (scallions), trimmed and
    chopped into long pieces
4cm/1½ in fresh root ginger, peeled and
    finely sliced
2 green or red Thai chillies, seeded and
    finely sliced

3 lemon grass stalks, finely sliced
a bunch of fresh dill, fronds chopped
1 bunch each of fresh basil and coriander
    (cilantro), stalks removed, leaves chopped
about 30ml/2 tbsp Thai fish sauce, plus extra,
    for serving
juice of 1 lemon
salt and ground black pepper

1 Clean the lobsters and crabs well and rub them with salt and pepper. Place half of them in a large steamer and pour the beer into the base.

2 Scatter half the spring onions, ginger, chillies, lemon grass and herbs over the lobsters and crabs, and steam for about 10 minutes, or until they turn red. Lift them on to a serving dish. Cook the remaining half in the same way.

3 Add the lemon grass, herbs and Thai fish sauce to the simmering beer, stir in the lemon juice, then pour into a dipping bowl. Serve the shellfish hot, dipping the lobster and crab meat into the broth and adding extra splashes of fish sauce, if you like.

COOK'S TIP
Whether you cook the lobsters and crabs at the same time depends on the number of people you are cooking for and the size of your steamer. However, they don't take long to cook so it is easy to steam them in batches.

Nutritional information per portion: Energy 264Kcal/1112kJ; Protein 48g; Carbohydrate 4g, of which sugars 1g; Fat 7g, of which saturates 1g; Cholesterol 210mg; Calcium 185mg; Fibre 0.5g; Sodium 1.3g.

Steamed mussels with celery

One of the best ways of preparing this classic dish is to simply steam the mussels in their own juices with celery and onions. This allows the delectable flavour of the mussels to shine through.

SERVES 4

4kg/9lb live mussels
40g/1½oz/3 tbsp butter, softened
2 onions, roughly chopped
3–4 celery sticks, roughly chopped
salt and ground white pepper
chopped fresh parsley, to garnish
French fries or crusty bread and pickles or
   mayonnaise, to serve

COOK'S TIP
The pan juices are delicious, so give diners spoons as well as bread for mopping them up.

1 Scrub the mussels until the shells are shiny black and smooth. Remove the beards, if present. If any of the shells are cracked or broken, discard them, along with any mussels that are open and that do not snap shut when tapped.

2 Melt the butter in a large heavy pan over medium heat. Add the onions and sauté for 5 minutes until softened and glazed. Add the celery and sauté for 5 minutes more. Add the mussels and season with salt and pepper.

3 Cover the pan and place over high heat for 3–4 minutes or until the mussels open, shaking the pan occasionally to distribute the steam.

4 Discard any mussels that have failed to open. Taste the liquid in the pan and adjust the seasoning if necessary, then spoon the mussels and the liquid into bowls or pots.

5 Sprinkle with parsley and serve with fries or crusty bread. Offer pickles, mayonnaise or mustard vinaigrette on the side.

Nutritional information per portion: Energy 393kcal/1658kJ; Protein 46.5g; Carbohydrate 17.3g, of which sugars 6g; Fat 15.5g, of which saturates 6.2g; Cholesterol 181mg; Calcium 183mg; Fibre 1.9g; Sodium 1048mg.

Mackerel escabeche

This traditional way of preserving fish in vinegar is a favourite in Latin America. Oily fish, such as mackerel and sardines, work particularly well. It takes at least a day, so allow plenty of time.

SERVES 6

12 small mackerel fillets
juice of 2 limes
90ml/6 tbsp olive oil
2 red onions, thinly sliced
2 garlic cloves, thinly sliced
2 bay leaves
6 black peppercorns
120ml/4fl oz/½ cup red wine vinegar
50g/2oz/½ cup plain (all-purpose) flour
salt and ground black pepper

1 Place the mackerel fillets side by side in a large, shallow glass or china dish. Pour over the lime juice. Season with salt and pepper and cover. Marinate in the refrigerator for 20–30 minutes, but no longer.

2 Meanwhile, heat half the oil in a frying pan. Add the onions and cook over a low heat for 10 minutes, until softened but not coloured. Stir in the garlic and cook for 2 minutes. Add the bay leaves, peppercorns and vinegar to the pan and simmer over a very low heat for 5 minutes.

3 Dry the mackerel fillets and coat in the flour. Heat the remaining oil in a frying pan and fry the fish, in batches, for 2 minutes on each side.

4 Return the fish to the dish in which they were marinated. Pour the vinegar mixture over. Marinate for 24 hours before serving.

COOK'S TIP
If you want to keep the fish for longer, immerse it in the vinegar, then top with a thin layer of olive oil. Covered tightly, it will keep in the refrigerator for 2 weeks.

Nutritional information per portion: Energy 518kcal/ 2147kJ; Protein 30g; Carbohydrate 11g, of which sugars 3g; Fat 39g, of which saturates 7g; Cholesterol 81mg; Calcium 42mg; Fibre 1g; Sodium 97mg.

Moroccan grilled fish brochettes

Serve these delicious skewers with grilled vegetables, which can be cooked on the barbecue alongside the fish brochettes. Accompany with warm flatbreads.

SERVES 4–6

5 garlic cloves, chopped

2.5ml/½ tsp paprika

2.5ml/½ tsp ground cumin

2.5–5ml/½–1 tsp salt

2–3 pinches of cayenne pepper

60ml/4 tbsp olive oil

30ml/2 tbsp lemon juice

30ml/2 tbsp chopped fresh coriander
(cilantro) or parsley

675g/1½ lb firm-fleshed white fish, such
as haddock, halibut, sea bass, snapper
or turbot, cut into cubes

3–4 green (bell) peppers, cut into
2.5–5cm/1–2in pieces

2 lemon wedges, to serve

1 Put the garlic, paprika, cumin, salt, cayenne pepper, oil, lemon juice and fresh coriander or parsley in a large bowl and mix together. Add the fish and toss to coat. Leave to marinate for at least 30 minutes, preferably 2 hours, at room temperature, or chill overnight in the refrigerator.

2 About 40 minutes before you are going to cook the brochettes, light the barbecue.

3 Meanwhile, thread the fish cubes and pepper pieces alternately on to wooden or metal skewers.

4 When the coals are ready, grill the brochettes on the barbecue for 2–3 minutes on each side, or until the fish is tender and lightly browned.

5 Transfer to a warmed serving plate. Serve with lemon wedges for squeezing over the brochettes.

Nutritional information per portion: Energy 276kcal/1157kJ; Protein 33.3g; Carbohydrate 8g, of which sugars 7.6g; Fat 12.5g, of which saturates 1.9g; Cholesterol 61mg; Calcium 34mg; Fibre 2g; Sodium 118mg.

Salmon and scallop lemon grass brochettes

Using lemon grass as skewers isn't a culinary gimmick, it gives a subtle but distinctive flavour to the ingredients – and, in this case, the fragrance goes perfectly with the salmon and scallops.

SERVES 4

8 lemon grass stalks

225g/8oz salmon fillet, skinned and cut into twelve similar-sized cubes

8 queen scallops, with their corals if possible

8 baby onions, peeled and blanched

1/2 yellow (bell) pepper, cut into eight squares

100g/4oz/1/2 cup butter

juice of 1/2 lemon

30ml/2 tbsp dry vermouth

5ml/1 tsp chopped fresh tarragon

salt, ground white pepper and paprika

1 Preheat the grill (broiler) to medium-high. Cut off the top 7.5–10cm/3–4in of each lemon grass stalk. Reserve the bulb ends for another dish.

2 Thread the salmon, scallops, corals if available, onions and pepper squares on to the lemon grass sticks and arrange the brochettes side by side in a grill (broiler) pan.

3 Melt half the butter in a small pan, add the lemon juice and a pinch of paprika and then brush all over the brochettes.

4 Grill (broil) the skewers for about 2–3 minutes on each side, turning and basting, until the fish and scallops are just cooked. Transfer to a platter and keep hot.

5 Pour the dry vermouth and the leftover cooking juices from the brochettes into a pan and boil fiercely to reduce by half. Add the remaining butter, stirring all the time. Stir in the tarragon and add salt and white pepper to taste.

6 Pour the tarragon butter sauce over the brochettes and serve.

Nutritional information per portion: Energy 336kcal/1391kJ; Protein 17g; Carbohydrate 7g, of which sugars 5g; Fat 27g, of which saturates 14g; Cholesterol 90mg; Calcium 40mg; Fibre 1g; Sodium 212mg.

Grilled red mullet with bay leaves

Red mullet have a lovely delicate, pale pink colour. They are simple to cook on a barbecue, with bay leaves for flavour and a drizzle of tangy dressing instead of a marinade.

SERVES 4

4 red mullet or snapper, 225–275g/
   8–10oz each, cleaned and descaled
olive oil, for brushing
fresh herb sprigs, such as fennel, dill,
   parsley, or thyme
2–3 dozen fresh or dried bay leaves

FOR THE DRESSING

90ml/6 tbsp olive oil
6 garlic cloves, finely chopped
$\frac{1}{2}$ dried chilli, seeded and chopped
juice of $\frac{1}{2}$ lemon
15ml/1 tbsp chopped parsley

1 Prepare the barbecue or preheat the grill (broiler) with the shelf 15cm/6in from the heat source.

2 Brush each fish with oil and stuff the cavities with the herb sprigs.

3 Brush the grill with oil and lay bay leaves across the cooking rack. Place the fish on top and cook for 15–20 minutes through, turning once.

4 To make the dressing, heat the olive oil in a pan and fry the garlic with the dried chilli. Add the lemon juice then strain into a bowl. Stir in the parsley. Serve the mullet drizzled with dressing.

COOK'S TIP

If you are cooking on the barbecue, the fish do not need to be descaled.

Nutritional information per portion: Energy 451kcal/1876kJ; Protein 38g; Carbohydrate 1g, of which sugars 0g; Fat 33g, of which saturates 4g; Cholesterol 0mg; Calcium 135mg; Fibre 0g; Sodium 183mg.

Salmon with light hollandaise and asparagus

This summery dish is light and colourful. The delicate flavour of asparagus makes the ideal accompaniment for salmon, and the hollandaise adds a luxurious texture.

SERVES 4

bunch of 20 asparagus spears, trimmed
4 salmon portions, such as steaks, about
    200g/7oz each
15ml/1 tbsp olive oil
juice of ½ lemon
25g/1oz/2 tbsp butter
salt and ground black pepper

FOR THE HOLLANDAISE SAUCE
45ml/3 tbsp white wine vinegar
6 peppercorns
1 bay leaf
3 egg yolks
175g/6oz/³/₄ cup butter, softened

1 Stand the asparagus in a deep pan. Blanch in salted boiling water for about 1 minute, then remove from the pan and refresh under cold running water. Drain.

2 To make the hollandaise sauce: in a small pan, boil the vinegar and 15ml/1 tbsp water with the peppercorns and bay leaf until reduced to 15ml/1 tbsp. Set aside.

3 Cream the egg yolks with 15g/½oz/1 tbsp butter and a pinch of salt. Strain the vinegar into the eggs and set the bowl over a pan of just-boiled water.

4 Off the heat, whisk in the remaining butter, no more than a teaspoon at a time, until the sauce is shiny and thick. Season to taste.

5 Heat a griddle pan or grill (broiler). Brush the salmon with olive oil, sprinkle with the lemon juice and season with salt and black pepper. Cook the fish on a high heat for 3–5 minutes on each side, depending on its thickness.

6 Melt the butter in a separate large pan and gently reheat the asparagus in it for 1–2 minutes before serving with the fish and hollandaise sauce.

Nutritional information per portion: Energy 834Kcal/3449kJ; Protein 46.5g; Carbohydrate 2.8g, of which sugars 2.7g; Fat 7.7g, of which saturates 31.6g; Cholesterol 358mg; Calcium 102mg; Fibre 2.1g; Sodium 401mg.

Grilled sole with chive butter

The very best way of transforming simply grilled fish into a luxury dish is by topping it with a flavoured butter, as in this recipe. Sole has a lovely, delicate flavour and texture.

SERVES 4

115g/4oz/½ cup unsalted butter, softened, plus
    extra, melted
5ml/1 tsp diced lemon grass
a pinch of finely grated lime rind
1 kaffir lime leaf, very finely shredded (optional)
45ml/3 tbsp chopped chives

2.5–5ml/½–1 tsp Thai fish sauce
4 sole, skinned
salt and ground black pepper
chopped chives or chive flowers, to garnish
lemon or lime wedges, to serve

1 Put the butter in a bowl and cream it with a wooden spoon. Add the lemon grass, lime rind, lime leaf, if using, and chives or chive flowers. Mix well, making sure all the ingredients are thoroughly combined, then season to taste with Thai fish sauce, salt and pepper.

2 Chill the butter mixture to firm it a little, then form it into a roll and wrap in foil or clear film (plastic wrap). Chill until firm. Preheat the grill (broiler).

3 Brush the fish with melted butter. Place it on the grill (broiling) rack and season. Grill (broil) for about 5 minutes on one side.

4 Carefully turn the pieces of fish over and grill the other side for 4–5 minutes, until the fish is firm and just cooked. Test the flesh with a fork; it should flake easily.

5 Meanwhile, cut the chilled butter into thin slices. Put the fish on individual plates and top with the butter. Garnish with chives and serve with lemon or lime wedges.

COOK'S TIPS
Finer white fish fillets, such as plaice, can be cooked in this way, but reduce the cooking time slightly.
The flavoured butter can be made ahead and frozen.

Nutritional information per portion: Energy 349kcal/1447kJ; Protein 27.4g; Carbohydrate 0.5g, of which sugars 0.5g; Fat 26.3g, of which saturates 15g; Cholesterol 136mg; Calcium 49mg; Fibre 0g; Sodium 591mg.

Umbrian stuffed grilled trout

This is a very simple Italian recipe for trout from Umbria, a landlocked region that relies on freshwater fish from the rivers and lakes, and where fresh river trout are highly prized.

SERVES 2

2 medium-sized trout, cleaned and gutted
120ml/8 tbsp soft breadcrumbs
juice of 1 lemon
150ml/10 tbsp extra virgin olive oil, plus
    extra for brushing
30ml/2 tbsp chopped fresh flat leaf
    parsley
sea salt and ground black pepper

1 Light the barbecue and wait until you have a heap of hot embers. Position the grill rack.

2 In a small bowl, mix the breadcrumbs with the lemon juice, half the olive oil and the parsley, and season well with salt and pepper. Stuff the inside of each trout with this mixture.

3 Score each trout lightly on each side through the skin, and rub the remaining oil all over the fish. Lay the fish on the grill rack and cook for about 10 minutes on each side, until cooked through, brushing with more oil during the cooking process.

4 Serve while still hot, removing the fillets from the fish at the table.

Nutritional information per portion: Energy 661kcal/2761kJ; Protein 40.9g; Carbohydrate 34.9g, of which sugars 1.2g; Fat 40.7g, of which saturates 6.2g; Cholesterol 147mg; Calcium 114mg; Fibre 1g; Sodium 475mg.

Trout de Navarra

This trout dish comes from the Spanish region of Navarre and features tender fish wrapped in slices of cured Serrano ham, the delicious Spanish version of prosciutto.

SERVES 4

4 brown or rainbow trout, about 250g/9oz each, cleaned
50g/2oz/ ¼ cup melted butter, plus extra for greasing
16 thin slices Serrano ham, about 200g/7oz
salt and ground black pepper
buttered potatoes, to serve (optional)

1 Preheat the grill (broiler) to high, with a shelf in the top position. Line a baking tray with foil and grease it with a little butter.

2 Working with the fish on the foil, fold a piece of ham into each belly. Reserve the eight best slices of ham for wrapping.

3 Brush each trout with a little butter, seasoning the outside lightly with salt and ground black pepper. Wrap two slices of ham around each one, crossways, tucking the ends into the belly of the fish.

4 Grill (broil) the trout for about 4 minutes, then carefully turn them over with a metal spatula, rolling them across on the belly, so the ham wrapping does not come loose, and grill for a further 4 minutes until the fish are cooked through – the flesh will flake easily when tested with the tip of a knife.

5 Serve the trout very hot, with any spare butter spooned over the top and around the sides. Diners should open the trout on their plates, and eat them from the inside, pushing the flesh off the skin.

Nutritional information per portion: Energy 369kcal/1546kJ; Protein 48g; Carbohydrate 0.6g, of which sugars 0.6g; Fat 19.4g, of which saturates 8.8g; Cholesterol 216mg; Calcium 66mg; Fibre 0g; Sodium 821mg.

Trout with curried orange butter

This recipe is perfect for midweek meals, as it takes around 20 minutes to prepare. You can make the butter in advance and keep it in the fridge for up to a week.

SERVES 4

25g/1oz/2 tbsp butter, softened
5ml/1 tsp curry powder
5ml/1 tsp grated orange rind
4 small trout, cleaned and gutted, heads removed
vegetable or sunflower oil, for brushing
rosemary sprigs
salt and ground black pepper
orange wedges, to garnish
new potatoes, to serve

1 Mix the softened butter, curry powder and orange rind together in a bowl with salt and plenty of ground black pepper. Wrap in foil and freeze for 10 minutes.

2 Brush the fish all over with oil and sprinkle well with salt and black pepper. Make three diagonal slashes through the skin and flesh on each side of the fish.

3 Cut the chilled flavoured butter into small pieces and carefully tuck inside the slashes in the fish.

4 Place the fish on a pre-heated griddle or a hot barbecue, scatter with rosemary sprigs, and cook for 3–4 minutes on each side, depending on the size of the fish. Garnish with wedges of orange and serve with new potatoes.

Nutritional information per portion: Energy 354kcal/1481kJ; Protein 44g; Carbohydrate 0g, of which sugars 0g; Fat 20g, of which saturates 6g; Cholesterol 164mg; Calcium 45mg; Fibre 0g; Sodium 141mg

Thai marinated sea trout

Sea trout has a superb texture and a flavour like that of wild salmon. It is best served with strong but complementary flavours, such as chillies and lime, that cut the richness of its flesh.

SERVES 6

6 sea trout cutlets, each about 115g/4oz, or wild or farmed salmon

2 garlic cloves, chopped

1 fresh long red chilli, seeded and chopped

45ml/3 tbsp chopped Thai basil

15ml/1 tbsp palm sugar (jaggery)

grated zest and juice of 1 lime

400ml/14fl oz/1²/₃ cups coconut milk

15ml/1 tbsp Thai fish sauce

2 limes, cut into wedges, for serving

COOK'S TIP

If you can't find palm sugar, replace it with the same amount of muscovado (brown) sugar.

1 Place the trout cutlets in a dish. Using a pestle, pound the garlic and chilli in a mortar. Add 30ml/2 tbsp of the Thai basil with the sugar and continue to pound to a rough paste.

2 Mix the lime zest and juice into the chilli paste, with the coconut milk. Pour over the cutlets. Cover and chill for 1 hour.

3 Remove the cutlets from the marinade and place them in an oiled hinged wire fish basket or directly on a lightly oiled grill.

4 Cook the fish for 4 minutes on each side.

5 Transfer the marinade to a small pan and bring to the boil, then simmer gently for 5 minutes, stirring, until slightly thickened. Add the Thai fish sauce and the remaining Thai basil.

6 Lift each fish cutlet on to a plate, pour over the sauce and serve with the lime wedges.

Nutritional information per portion: Energy 174kcal/735kJ; Protein 23g; Carbohydrate 7g, of which sugars 6g; Fat 6g, of which saturates 1g; Cholesterol 77mg; Calcium 48mg; Fibre 0g; Sodium 230mg.

Grilled squid stuffed with feta

This way of cooking squid makes the most of their tender flesh, by marinating and then grilling on a hot barbecue. Serve with some fried potatoes for a main course, or alone as an appetizer.

SERVES 4

4 medium squid, total weight about 900g/2lb
4–8 finger-length slices of feta cheese
90ml/6 tbsp olive oil
2 garlic cloves, crushed
3–4 fresh marjoram sprigs, leaves removed and chopped, plus extra to garnish
salt and ground black pepper
lemon wedges, to serve

1 Prepare the squid, following the instructions on page 68. Rinse them thoroughly, inside and out, and drain well. Lay the squid bodies and tentacles in a shallow dish that will hold them in a single layer. Tuck the pieces of cheese between the squid.

2 To make the marinade, pour the oil into a bowl and whisk in the garlic and marjoram. Season.

3 Pour the marinade over the squid and cheese, cover and marinate in the refrigerator for 2–3 hours, turning once. Light the barbecue.

4 Place two pieces of cheese and leaves of marjoram from the marinade in each squid and place on a lightly oiled grill over the coals. Thread the tentacles on skewers.

5 Grill the stuffed squid for about 6 minutes, then turn them over. Grill them for 1–2 minutes more, then add the skewered tentacles. Grill them for 2 minutes on each side, until they start to scorch.

6 Serve the stuffed squid with the tentacles. Add a few lemon wedges, for squeezing over the seafood.

Nutritional information per portion: Energy 512kcal/2133kJ; Protein 43g; Carbohydrate 4g, of which sugars 1g; Fat 36g, of which saturates 11g; Cholesterol 541mg; Calcium 215mg; Fibre 0g; Sodium 968mg.

Grilled tamarind prawns

These succulent prawns are flavoured with tamarind, which gives a lovely sour taste that is balanced by the sugar in the marinade.

SERVES 2–4

500g/1¼ lb fresh, large prawns (shrimp), deveined, legs and feelers removed
45ml/3 tbsp tamarind pulp
30ml/2 tbsp dark soy sauce
15ml/1 tbsp sugar
ground black pepper
fresh coriander (cilantro) leaves and 2–4 green chillies, seeded and quartered lengthways, to garnish

1 Rinse the prawns, pat dry and make an incision along the curve of the tail with a sharp knife.

2 Put the tamarind pulp in a bowl and add 250ml/8fl oz/1 cup warm water. Soak, squeezing with your fingers to help soften it. Strain the liquid and discard any fibres.

3 In a bowl, mix together the tamarind juice, soy sauce, sugar and black pepper.

4 Pour the mixture over the prawns, rubbing it into the incision in the tails. Cover marinate for 1 hour.

5 Prepare the charcoal, or heat the conventional grill (broiler), and place the prawns on the rack. Grill (broil) for about 3 minutes on each side until cooked through, brushing them with the marinade as they cook.

6 Serve the prawns hot, garnished with coriander and chillies.

Nutritional information per portion: Energy 74Kcal/309kJ; Protein 11.4g; Carbohydrate 4.9g, of which sugars 4.8g; Fat 1.1g, of which saturates 0.3g; Cholesterol 39mg; Calcium 97mg; Fibre 0.6g; Sodium 1301mg.

Fried and Baked

The preferred way of cooking fish the

world over, is frying – either in a light,

crisp batter, or quickly pan-fried in

butter or olive oil. It is certainly the

speediest method, and one that suits

the delicate flesh. Baking fish is

another good way to retain moisture,

and in this chapter you will find some

truly fabulous fried and baked dishes for

all types of fish and shellfish.

Fish and chips

This is one of England's national dishes. Cook in batches so that each piece of fish and all the chips are perfectly crisp. Salt and vinegar are the traditional accompaniments.

SERVES 4

115g/4oz/1 cup self-raising
   (self-rising) flour
150ml/¼ pint/²/₃ cup water
675g/1½ lb potatoes, peeled and cut
   into chips about 1cm/½ in wide and
   5cm/2in long
oil, for deep frying
675g/1½ lb skinned cod fillet,
   cut into four pieces
salt and pepper
lemon wedges, to serve

1 Place the flour and salt in a bowl. Make a well in the centre. Whisk in the water to make a smooth batter. Leave for 30 minutes.

2 Put the chipped potatoes in a colander and rinse them with cold water, then drain and dry well.

3 Heat the oil in a deep-fat fryer or large heavy pan to 150°C/300°F. Using a wire basket, lower the chips in batches into the hot oil and cook for 5–6 minutes, shaking the basket occasionally until soft but not browned. Remove from the oil and drain them on kitchen paper.

4 Increase the heat of the oil in the fryer to 190°C/375°F. Season the pieces of fish with salt and pepper. Stir the batter, then dip the fish into it, one piece at a time, allowing the excess to drain off.

5 Working in two batches, lower the fish into the hot oil and fry for 6–8 minutes, until crisp and brown. Drain on kitchen paper and keep warm.

6 Make sure the oil is hot again then add a batch of chips, frying for 2–3 minutes, until crisp. Keep hot while cooking the other batches. Sprinkle with salt and serve with the fish.

Nutritional information per portion: Energy 521kcal/2188kJ; Protein 36.3g; Carbohydrate 48.9g, of which sugars 2.6g; Fat 21.3g, of which saturates 2.7g; Cholesterol 78mg; Calcium 126mg; Fibre 2.6g; Sodium 223mg.

Halibut fillets with parsley sauce

This is a favourite dish in Denmark, where, in the past, Norsemen considered halibut 'the fish of the gods' and a holy fish. It is traditionally served with shredded greens.

SERVES 4

2 eggs, beaten
10ml/2 tsp water
75g/3oz/1½ cup fine breadcrumbs
900g/2lb halibut fillet, cut into four
   pieces
10ml/2 tsp salt
2.5ml/½ tsp white pepper
50g/2oz/4 tbsp butter
4 lemon wedges, to garnish
shredded greens, or other seasonal
   vegetable, to serve

FOR THE PARSLEY SAUCE
50g/2oz/4 tbsp butter
60ml/4 tbsp plain (all-purpose) flour
350ml/12fl oz/1½ cups milk
45ml/3 tbsp chopped fresh parsley
salt

1 Whisk the eggs and water together in a shallow dish. Place the breadcrumbs in a second dish. Dip the fish into the egg mixture, then into the breadcrumbs, to coat both sides evenly. Sprinkle with salt and pepper. Allow the fish to rest for at least 10 minutes before cooking it.

2 To make the parsley sauce, melt the butter in a pan over a medium heat, and whisk in the flour. Reduce the heat and cook the roux for 3–5 minutes until pale beige. Slowly add the milk; cook, whisking constantly, until it comes to a gentle boil.

3 Season the thickened sauce, add the parsley and simmer for 2 minutes. Cover and keep warm.

4 To cook the fish, melt the butter in a large pan over a medium heat. When the butter is foaming, place the halibut fillets in the pan, and cook for about 4 minutes on each side, turning once, until the coating is golden brown and the fish flakes easily with a fork.

5 Serve the halibut fillets with the sauce spooned over, accompanied by freshly cooked vegetables.

Nutritional information per portion: Energy 594kcal/2493kJ; Protein 58.2g; Carbohydrate 30.4g, of which sugars 5g; Fat 27.6g, of which saturates 14.1g; Cholesterol 227mg; Calcium 234mg; Fibre 0.9g; Sodium 487mg.

Halibut with leek and ginger

The flesh of halibut can be very tender: it is white and firm, and has a good flavour. When buying steaks, however, it is best to avoid the tail end, where there is more bone than flesh.

SERVES 4

2 leeks, trimmed, and cut into 5cm/
   2in lengths
50g/2oz piece fresh root ginger, peeled,
   thinly sliced and then cut into thin
   sticks
4 halibut steaks, approximately 175g/6oz
   each
15ml/1 tbsp olive oil
75g/3oz/6 tbsp butter
mashed potato, to serve

1 Cut the lengths of leeks in half lengthways, then slice into thin matchsticks. Wash thoroughly.

2 Dry the halibut steaks on kitchen paper. Heat a large pan with the olive oil and add 50g/2oz/¼ cup of the butter. As it begins to bubble, place the fish steaks carefully in the pan, skin side down.

3 Allow the halibut to colour – this will take 3–4 minutes. Then turn the steaks over, reduce the heat and cook for a further 10 minutes.

4 Remove the fish from the pan, set aside and keep warm. Add the leek and ginger to the pan, stir to mix then allow the leek to soften (they may colour slightly, but this is fine). Once softened, season with a little salt and ground black pepper.

5 Cut the remaining butter into small pieces, then, off the heat, gradually stir into the pan.

6 Serve the halibut steaks with the leek and ginger mixture and accompanied by mashed potato.

Nutritional information per portion: Energy 364kcal/1520kJ; Protein 39.1g; Carbohydrate 2.7g, of which sugars 2.1g; Fat 21.9g, of which saturates 10.8g; Cholesterol 101mg; Calcium 75mg; Fibre 1.9g; Sodium 221mg.

Fried fish with shellfish sauce

A luxurious way of enhancing the simplicity of fried fish is to serve it with a lavish amount of shellfish in a wine-flavoured sauce. This dish is both impressive and delicious.

SERVES 6

12 mussels, cleaned, discarding any open
    mussles that fail to close when tapped
12 cockles
12 clams
6 small squid, cleaned and sliced
12 king prawns (jumbo shrimp), deveined
12 scallops, sliced
6 white fish fillets, such as sea bass,
    haddock or sole
50g/2oz plain (all-purpose) flour
250ml/8fl oz/1 cup vegetable oil
1 large red onion, diced
15ml/1 tbsp chilli sauce
5ml/1 tsp paprika
2.5ml/½ tsp ground cumin
1 glass white wine
salt and ground black pepper
lime wedges and boiled potatoes or rice,
    to serve

1 Put the mussels in a pan with a little water. Bring to the boil, cover, and cook until opened. Drain, discarding any that fail to open after about 5 minutes. Using a teaspoon, detach the flesh from the shells. Discard the shells. Steam and shell the cockles and clams, separately, in the same way.

2 Season the fish fillets and dust with flour. Heat the oil in a frying pan, reserving 30–45ml/2–3 tbsp, and fry over a high heat, turning once, until golden and cooked through. Keep warm.

3 Heat the remaining oil in a large pan over medium heat and fry the onion for about 10 minutes, until golden brown. Stir in the chilli sauce, paprika and cumin and season well.

4 Add all prepared shellfish to the pan and cook, stirring, for 2 minutes, then add the wine, cover the pan and simmer for about 5 minutes.

5 Pour the seafood sauce over the fried fish and serve immediately, with lime wedges to squeeze over the fish, and accompanied by rice or boiled potatoes.

Nutritional information per portion: Energy 343kcal/1429kJ; Protein 31.1g; Carbohydrate 9.1g, of which sugars 0.9g; Fat 18.4g, of which saturates 2g; Cholesterol 133mg; Calcium 86mg; Fibre 0.4g; Sodium 668mg.

Fish fillets in creamy mustard sauce

This dish is from northern Germany. You can use any kind of firm, white fish, or a mix of different kinds. Fried potatoes with bacon and onions are a perfect accompaniment.

SERVES 4

300ml/½ pint/1¼ cups fish stock

100ml/3½ oz/scant ½ cup single (light) cream

10ml/2 tsp grainy mustard

1kg/2¼lb boiled potatoes, thinly sliced

150g/5oz bacon, diced into cubes

1 onion, finely chopped

a small bunch of chives, chopped

800g/1¾lb fish fillets (cod, salmon, trout, pike or perch)

juice of 1 lemon

oil, for frying

salt and ground white pepper

fresh dill, to garnish

1 Heat the fish stock and season to taste with salt and pepper. Add the cream and mustard and simmer for 5 minutes to make the sauce.

2 Heat some oil in a frying pan over high heat and fry the potato slices and the bacon until browned and crisp. Add the onion and fry for another 5 minutes. Season with salt and pepper and stir in the chives.

3 Meanwhile, season the fish with lemon juice, salt and pepper.

4 Heat some oil in another pan and fry the fillets, turning once, until golden on both sides.

5 Arrange the potatoes on a serving plate with the fish round them and pour the sauce around. Garnish with fresh dill.

Nutritional information per portion: Energy 570kcal/2387kJ; Protein 47.9g; Carbohydrate 42.5g, of which sugars 5.1g; Fat 24.1g, of which saturates 6.9g; Cholesterol 126mg; Calcium 62mg; Fibre 2.7g; Sodium 738mg.

Fish in tangy tomato sauce

This fried fish dish from the Assam region of India is quick and easy to put together, and makes a refreshing, healthy and delicious choice for a dinner. Any firm white fish can be used.

SERVES 4

675g/1½ lb fillets of tilapia, monkfish or other firm white fish

1 tsp ground turmeric

1 tsp salt or to taste

3 tbsp mustard oil

½ tsp black mustard seeds

½ tsp nigella seeds

10–12 fenugreek seeds

2 green chillies, sliced lengthways, and seeded if you prefer

2 small potatoes, about 200g/7oz, finely chopped

250ml/8fl oz/1 cup warm water

400g/14oz chopped canned tomatoes, with their juice

1 tbsp lime juice

1 tbsp chopped fresh coriander (cilantro) leaves

plain boiled rice, to serve

1 Cut the fish into 5cm/2in pieces and lay them on a large plate. Sprinkle half of the turmeric and half the salt over them and rub both gently into the fish.

2 Heat the oil over a medium to high heat until it starts to smoke but not burn, then fry the fish fillets in batches until the edges turn brown. Drain the fish pieces on absorbent kitchen paper.

3 Take the pan off the heat and add the mustard seeds, nigella seeds and fenugreek seeds, followed by the chillies. Return the pan to the heat.

4 Add the potatoes to the pan. Fry these together until the potatoes are golden brown.

5 Add the remaining turmeric and salt, and pour in 250ml/8fl oz/1 cup warm water. Bring the pan to the boil, reduce the heat to low and cook for a further 5–6 minutes.

6 Add the tomatoes to the pan and cook for another 5 minutes. Next, add the fried fish and cook for 5 minutes. Stir in the lime juice and coriander and remove from the heat. Serve with a large spoonful of plain boiled rice.

Nutritional information per portion: Energy 345kcal/1445kJ; Protein 23g; Carbohydrate 28.3g, of which sugars 5.6g; Fat 16.3g, of which saturates 4.2g; Cholesterol 144mg; Calcium 105mg; Fibre 2g; Sodium 338mg.

Fried fish with onion and tomato sauce

This dish comes from Peru, where it is often cooked and sold on the harbour sides of coastal towns, using the newly delivered catch that the fishing boats have brought in that morning.

SERVES 6

6 white fish fillets, such as cod, haddock or sea bass

50g/2oz plain (all-purpose) flour

250ml/8fl oz/1 cup vegetable oil

3 medium red onions, sliced into rings

3 garlic cloves, finely chopped

4 tomatoes, peeled, seeded and diced

2 chillies, seeded and sliced lengthways

15ml/1 tbsp chilli sauce

2.5ml/½ tsp dried oregano

juice of 1 lime

salt and ground black pepper

parsley leaves, to garnish

rice or boiled potatoes, to serve

1 Season the fish with salt and pepper and dust with flour. Heat the oil in a frying pan, reserving 30ml/ 2 tbsp, and fry the fillets, turning once, until golden and cooked through. Transfer the fish to a plate and keep warm.

2 Heat the reserved oil over medium heat and fry the onions until they are browned.

3 Add the garlic, tomatoes, chilli strips, chilli sauce and the oregano to the pan, and cook for 5 minutes.

4 Spoon the onion and tomato mixture into a serving dish and lay the fish on top, or transfer the sauce to a bowl and serve on the side. Sprinkle the fish with lime juice and garnish with parsley. Serve with rice or boiled potatoes.

Nutritional information per portion: Energy 345kcal/1445kJ; Protein 23g; Carbohydrate 28.3g, of which sugars 5.6g; Fat 16.3g, of which saturates 4.2g; Cholesterol 144mg; Calcium 105mg; Fibre 2g; Sodium 338mg.

Pan-fried red mullet with basil and citrus

Red mullet is popular all over the Mediterranean. This Italian recipe combines it with oranges and lemons, which grow in abundance in the south of the country.

SERVES 4

4 red mullet or snapper, weighing about
    225g/8oz each, filleted
90ml/6 tbsp olive oil
10 peppercorns, crushed
2 oranges, one peeled and sliced, and one
    squeezed
1 lemon, halved, zest removed and thinly
    sliced from one half, juice squeezed
    from the other
plain (all purpose) flour, for dusting
15g/½oz/1 tbsp butter
2 canned anchovies, drained and chopped
60ml/4 tbsp shredded fresh basil
salt and ground black pepper

1 Place the fish fillets in a shallow glass or china dish in a single layer. Pour over the olive oil and sprinkle with the crushed peppercorns. Arrange the orange slices on top of the fish. Cover and marinate in the refrigerator for at least 4 hours.

2 Lift the fish out of the marinade and dry on kitchen paper. Reserve the marinade and orange slices. Season the fish and dust with flour.

3 Heat 45ml/3 tbsp of the marinade in a frying pan. Add the fish and fry for 2 minutes on each side.

4 Remove from the pan and keep warm. Discard the residue in the pan and wipe clean.

5 Melt the butter in the pan with any of the remaining original marinade. Add the anchovies and cook, stirring, until completely softened and mashed.

6 Stir in the orange and lemon juice, and sliced zest, then check the seasoning and simmer until slightly reduced. Stir in the basil. Pour the sauce over the fish. Serve with the orange and lemon slices.

Nutritional information per portion: Energy 328kcal/1364kJ; Protein 24.5g; Carbohydrate 0.4g, of which sugars 0.3g; Fat 25.5g, of which saturates 2.9g; Cholesterol 0mg; Calcium 123mg; Fibre 1g; Sodium 411mg.

Livorno-style red mullet

The ancient Italian port of Livorno, on the western coast of Tuscany, is famous for its sweet red mullet. The smaller the mullet, the better the flavour.

SERVES 6

12 small red mullet or snapper, scaled, cleaned and gutted
30–45ml/2–3 tbsp plain (all-purpose) flour
75ml/5 tbsp olive oil
250ml/8fl oz/1 cup dry white wine
½ onion, finely chopped
1 garlic clove, chopped
1 bay leaf
a handful of flat leaf parsley, chopped
400g/14oz can tomatoes, strained and chopped
sea salt and ground black pepper

1 Dry the fish carefully inside and out with kitchen paper and coat them lightly with flour.

2 Heat the oil in a frying pan and fry the mullet for about 4 minutes.

3 Turn the fish over carefully, then add the dry white wine, chopped onion, chopped garlic, bay leaf, parsley and a little salt and pepper.

4 Shake the pan, then spoon the flavouring ingredients over the fish.

5 Allow the alcohol from the wine to evaporate for 1–2 minutes, then add the canned tomatoes.

6 Cover with a lid and simmer gently for a further 5 minutes. Serve the fish immediately.

Nutritional information per portion: Energy 279kcal/1165kJ; Protein 24.9g; Carbohydrate 5.7g, of which sugars 2.9g; Fat 14.7g, of which saturates 1.4g; Cholesterol 0mg; Calcium 106mg; Fibre 0.9g; Sodium 133mg.

Marinated fried fish with ginger and chilli

Fish and shellfish are a strong feature of the cuisine in the coastal region of southern India. Kerala, in the southernmost part of the country, produces some of the finest fish dishes.

SERVES 4–6

1 small onion, coarsely chopped

4 garlic cloves, crushed

5cm/2in piece fresh root ginger, chopped

5ml/1 tsp ground turmeric

10ml/2 tsp chilli powder

4 red mullet or snapper

vegetable oil, for shallow-frying

5ml/1 tsp cumin seeds

3 fresh green chillies, finely sliced

salt

lemon or lime wedges, to serve

1 In a food processor, grind the first five ingredients with a good pinch of salt to a smooth paste.

2 Make several slashes on both sides of the fish and rub them with the paste. Leave to rest for 1 hour. Excess fluid will be released as the salt dissolves, so lightly pat the fish dry with kitchen paper, without removing the paste.

3 Heat the oil and fry the cumin seeds and chillies for 1 minute.

4 Add the fish, in batches if necessary, and fry on one side. When the first side is sealed, turn them over very gently to ensure they do not break. Fry until golden brown on both sides and fully cooked. Drain and serve hot, with lemon or lime wedges.

Nutritional information per portion: Energy 335kcal/1406kJ; Protein 31.9g; Carbohydrate 18.4g, of which sugars 11.5g; Fat 15.5g, of which saturates 1.4g; Cholesterol 0mg; Calcium 166mg; Fibre 4.6g; Sodium 347mg.

Monkfish with pimiento and cream sauce

This recipe comes from the Rioja region of Spain, where a special horned red pepper grows and is used to make a spicy sauce. Here, red peppers are used with a little chilli, while the cream makes a mellow sauce. The perfect accompaniment to this is a glass of white Rioja.

SERVES 4

2 large red (bell) peppers
1kg/2¼lb monkfish tail or 900g/2lb halibut
plain (all-purpose) flour, for dusting
30ml/2 tbsp olive oil
25g/1oz/2 tbsp butter
120ml/4fl oz/½ cup white Rioja or
    dry vermouth

½ dried chilli, seeded and chopped
8 raw prawns (shrimp), in the shell
150ml/¼ pint/⅔ cup double (heavy) cream
salt and ground black pepper
fresh flat leaf parsley, to garnish

1 Preheat the grill (broiler) to high and cook the peppers for 8–12 minutes, turning occasionally, until they are soft, and the skins blackened. Leave, covered, until cool enough to handle. Remove the skin and discard the stalks and seeds. Put the flesh into a blender, strain in the juices and purée.

2 Cut the monkfish or halibut into eight steaks (freeze the bones for stock). Season well and dust with flour.

3 Heat the oil and butter in a large frying pan and fry the fish for 3 minutes on each side. Remove to a warm dish.

4 Add the wine or vermouth and chilli to the pan and stir to deglaze the pan. Add the prawns and cook them briefly, then lift out and reserve.

5 Boil the sauce to reduce by half, then strain into a small jug (pitcher). Add the cream to the pan and boil briefly to reduce. Return the sauce to the pan, stir in the puréed peppers and check the seasonings. Pour the sauce over the fish and serve, garnished with the cooked prawns and parsley.

Nutritional information per portion: Energy 500kcal/2087kJ; Protein 49.7g; Carbohydrate 7.2g, of which sugars 6.9g; Fat 27.1g, of which saturates 13.7g; Cholesterol 140mg; Calcium 70mg; Fibre 1.4g; Sodium 113mg.

Plaice fillets with sorrel and lemon butter

Sorrel is a wild herb that is now grown commercially. It is very good in salads and, roughly chopped, partners this slightly sweet-fleshed fish very well.

SERVES 4

200g/7oz/scant 1 cup butter
500g/1¼lb plaice fillets, skinned and patted dry
30ml/2 tbsp chopped fresh sorrel
90ml/6 tbsp dry white wine
a little lemon juice

COOK'S TIP
Sorrel has a sour, slightly acidic flavour. It should have bright green crisp leaves, and should not be used if the leaves are wilted or yellow. If you cannot find sorrel, you could try this recipe using tarragon or thyme instead.

1 Heat half the butter in a large frying pan and, just as it is melted, place the fillets skin side down. Cook briefly, just to firm up, reduce the heat and turn the fish over. The fish will be cooked in less than 5 minutes. Try not to let the butter brown or allow the fish to colour.

2 Remove the fish fillets from the pan and keep warm between two plates. Dice the remaining butter.

3 Add the chopped sorrel to the pan and stir. Add the wine, then, as it bubbles, add the diced butter, swirling it in piece by piece and not allowing the sauce to boil. Stir in a little lemon juice.

4 Serve the fish with the sorrel and lemon butter spooned over, accompanied by some crunchy green beans and perhaps some new potatoes, if you like.

Nutritional information per portion: Energy 494kcal/2047kJ; Protein 25.7g; Carbohydrate 0.5g, of which sugars 0.5g; Fat 43.3g, of which saturates 26.4g; Cholesterol 170mg; Calcium 98mg; Fibre 0.3g; Sodium 501mg.

Pan-fried sea bream with lime and tomato salsa

The most popular way of cooking a fresh piece of fish is to pan-fry it or grill it. In this recipe a simple salsa is briefly sizzled at the end of cooking, to make a light sauce.

SERVES 4

4 sea bream fillets
juice of 2 limes
30ml/2 tbsp chopped coriander (cilantro)
1 fresh red chilli, seeded and finely
   chopped
2 spring onions (scallions), sliced
45ml/3 tbsp olive oil, plus extra to serve
2 large tomatoes, diced
salt
cooked white rice, to serve

1 Place the fish fillets in a shallow china or glass dish large enough to hold them all in a single layer. Mix the lime juice, coriander, chilli and spring onions in a bowl. Stir in half the oil, then pour this marinade over the fish.

2 Cover and marinate for around 15–20 minutes. Do not be tempted to marinate the fish for longer than this or it will start to 'cook'.

3 Heat the remaining oil in a large frying pan over a high heat. Lift each piece of fish from the marinade and pat dry with kitchen paper.

4 Season the fish with salt and place in the hot pan, skin side down. Cook for 2 minutes, then turn and cook for a further 2 minutes, until the flesh is opaque all the way through.

5 Add the marinade and the chopped tomatoes to the pan. Bring the sauce to the boil and cook for about 1 minute, until the tomatoes are lightly cooked but still retain their shape.

6 Drizzle a little olive oil over the fish and serve on warm plates, with white rice and the tomato salsa.

Nutritional information per portion: Energy 166kcal/698kJ; Protein 27.3g; Carbohydrate 2g, of which sugars 2g; Fat 5.5g, of which saturates 0.2g; Cholesterol 57mg; Calcium 84mg; Fibre 1g; Sodium 173mg.

Sweet and sour snapper

Originating in the northern region of Shandong, China, this dish comprises a whole deep-fried fish served with a medley of vegetables.

SERVES 4

4 dried Chinese black mushrooms

1 whole snapper or similar fish, about 800g/1¾lb, cleaned and scaled

15ml/1 tbsp salt

45ml/3 tbsp cornflour (cornstarch)

oil for deep- and shallow-frying

15ml/1 tbsp thinly sliced root ginger

15ml/1 tbsp crushed garlic

1 spring onion, cut into 2.5cm/1in lengths, plus extra, to garnish

30ml/2 tbsp thinly sliced bamboo shoots

½ red (bell) pepper, thinly sliced

FOR THE SAUCE

60ml/4 tbsp white wine vinegar

15ml/1 tbsp sugar

15ml/1 tbsp light soy sauce

10ml/2 tsp cornflour (cornstarch) mixed with 45ml/3 tbsp water

200ml/7fl oz/scant 1 cup water or stock

1 Soak the mushrooms in boiling water for 20–30 minutes, until soft. Rinse the fish inside and out, then pat dry with kitchen paper. Make deep cuts diagonally across both sides of the fish. Rub with the salt, rinse and pat dry. Dust the fish with cornflour.

2 Heat the oil in a wok that is large enough to hold the fish comfortably. Carefully lower the fish into the oil and fry over medium heat for 7–8 minutes, until the skin is crisp and golden brown and the fish is cooked through. Remove it from the wok and drain on kitchen paper. Place the fish on a serving platter with a deep lip to hold the sauce, and keep hot.

3 Drain the mushrooms and slice them thinly, discarding the stems. In a clean wok, heat 30ml/2 tbsp oil and stir-fry the ginger and garlic for 1 minute. Add the spring onions, bamboo shoots and pepper, with the sliced mushrooms. Stir-fry for 2 minutes more.

4 Mix all the sauce ingredients in a bowl. Add to the wok, bring to the boil and simmer for 1 minute, until the sauce thickens. Pour over the fish and garnish with more spring onions. Serve immediately.

Nutritional information per portion: Energy 332kcal/1389kJ; Protein 25.4g; Carbohydrate 14.2g, of which sugars 1.1g; Fat 19.8g, of which saturates 2.6g; Cholesterol 46mg; Calcium 61mg; Fibre 0.2g; Sodium 884mg.

Trout with tamarind and chilli sauce

Sometimes trout, especially if it is farmed rather than wild, can taste rather bland, but this spicy sauce really gives it a zing. If you like your food very spicy, add an extra chilli.

SERVES 4

4 trout, cleaned
6 spring onions (scallions), sliced
60ml/4 tbsp soy sauce
15ml/1 tbsp vegetable oil
30ml/2 tbsp chopped fresh coriander
   (cilantro) and strips of chilli, to garnish

FOR THE SAUCE
50g/2oz tamarind pulp
105ml/7 tbsp boiling water
2 shallots, coarsely chopped
1 fresh red chilli, seeded and chopped
1cm/½ in piece fresh root ginger, peeled
   and chopped
5ml/1 tsp soft light brown sugar
45ml/3 tbsp Thai fish sauce

1 Slash the trout diagonally four or five times on each side. Place in a shallow dish in a single layer. Fill the cavity of each trout with spring onions and douse each fish with soy sauce. Turn the fish to coat both sides with the sauce. Sprinkle any remaining spring onions on the top.

2 To make the sauce, put the tamarind pulp in a bowl and pour over the boiling water. Mash with a fork until softened and combined, then transfer to a food processor.

3 Add the shallots, fresh chilli, ginger, sugar and fish sauce to the tamarind and process to a coarse pulp. Scrape into a bowl.

4 Heat the oil in a large frying pan and cook the trout, for about 5 minutes on each side, until the skin is crisp and browned.

5 Transfer the trout to serving plates and spoon over some of the sauce. Sprinkle with the coriander and chilli and serve with the remaining sauce.

Nutritional information per portion: Energy 82kcal/346kJ; Protein 12g; Carbohydrate 2g, of which sugars 1.6g; Fat 3g, of which saturates 0.6g; Cholesterol 48mg; Calcium 24mg; Fibre 0.3g; Sodium 245mg.

Cheese-topped trout

Succulent strips of filleted trout are topped with a mixture of Parmesan cheese, pine nuts, herbs and breadcrumbs before being drizzled with lemon butter and grilled.

SERVES 4

50g/2oz/1 cup fresh white breadcrumbs
50g/2oz Parmesan cheese, grated
25g/1oz/⅓ cup pine nuts, chopped
15ml/1 tbsp chopped fresh parsley
15ml/1 tbsp chopped fresh coriander
    (cilantro)
30ml/2 tbsp olive oil
4 thick trout fillets, about 225g/8oz each
40g/1½ oz/3 tbsp butter
juice of 1 lemon
salt and ground black pepper
lemon slices, to garnish
steamed baby asparagus and carrots,
    to serve

1 In a mixing bowl, combine the breadcrumbs, Parmesan cheese, pine nuts, parsley and coriander. Add the oil.

2 Cut each trout fillet into two strips. Firmly press the breadcrumb mixture on to the top of each strip of trout.

3 Preheat the grill (broiler) to high. Grease the grill (broiling) pan with 15g/1 tbsp of the butter.

4 Melt the remaining butter in a pan and stir in the lemon juice.

5 Place the breadcrumb-topped fillets on the greased grill pan and pour the lemon butter over.

6 Grill (broil) the trout for about 10 minutes or until the fillets are just cooked. Place two trout strips on each plate, garnish with lemon slices and serve with steamed asparagus and carrots.

Nutritional information per portion: Energy 524kcal/2185kJ; Protein 51.3g; Carbohydrate 10.3g, of which sugars 0.9g; Fat 31.1g, of which saturates 8.9g; Cholesterol 34mg; Calcium 214mg; Fibre 1g; Sodium 422mg.

Tuna steaks with red onion salsa

Red onions are ideal for this salsa, not only for their mild and sweet flavour, but also because they look so appetizing. A bowl of thick yogurt mixed with chopped herbs is a good accompaniment.

SERVES 4

4 tuna loin steaks, about
  175–200g/6–7oz each
5ml/1 tsp cumin seeds, toasted and
  crushed
a pinch of dried red chilli flakes
grated rind and juice of 1 lime
30–60ml/2–4 tbsp extra virgin olive oil
salt and ground black pepper
lime wedges and fresh coriander sprigs,
  to garnish

FOR THE SALSA

1 small red onion, finely chopped
200g/7oz red or yellow cherry tomatoes,
  roughly chopped
1 avocado, peeled, stoned (pitted) and
  chopped
2 kiwi fruit, peeled and chopped
1 fresh red chilli, seeded and finely
  chopped

15g/½ oz fresh coriander, chopped
6 fresh mint sprigs, leaves only, chopped
5–10ml/1–2 tsp Thai fish sauce
about 5ml/1 tsp muscovado
  (molasses) sugar

1 Wash the tuna steaks and pat dry. Sprinkle with half the cumin, the dried chilli, salt, pepper and half the lime rind. Rub in 30ml/2 tbsp of the oil and set aside in a glass or china dish for about 30 minutes.

2 To make the salsa, mix the chopped onion, tomatoes, avocado, kiwi fruit, chilli, coriander and mint in a bowl.

3 Add the remaining cumin, the rest of the lime rind and half the lime juice to the bowl. Add the fish sauce and sugar to taste. Leave for 15–20 minutes, then taste, and add more Thai fish sauce, lime juice and olive oil if required.

4 Heat a ridged, cast iron grill (griddle) pan. Cook the tuna, allowing about 2 minutes on each side for rare tuna or a little longer for a medium result.

5 Serve the tuna steaks garnished with lime wedges and coriander sprigs. Serve the salsa with the tuna.

Nutritional information per portion: Energy 389kcal/1628kJ; Protein 43.2g; Carbohydrate 7.9g, of which sugars 6.8g; Fat 20.7g, of which saturates 4.4g; Cholesterol 49mg; Calcium 55mg; Fibre 2.5g; Sodium 180mg.

Seared tuna with ginger and chilli

In this recipe the salad is served just warm as a bed for the tender tuna. The dash of fiery harissa paste creates a dish that will transport you to the warmth of the North African coastline.

SERVES 4

30ml/2 tbsp olive oil
5ml/1 tsp harissa
5ml/1 tsp clear honey
4 x 200g/7oz tuna steaks
salt and ground black pepper

FOR THE SALAD

30ml/2 tbsp olive oil
a little butter
25g/1oz fresh ginger, peeled and grated
2 garlic cloves, finely sliced
2 green chillies, seeded and finely sliced
6 spring onions (scallions), sliced
2 large handfuls of watercress
juice of ½ lemon

1 Mix the olive oil, harissa, honey and salt together in a bowl, and rub it over the tuna steaks.

2 Heat a frying pan, grease it with a little oil and sear the tuna steaks for about 2 minutes on each side. They should still be pink on the inside.

3 Keep the tuna warm while you quickly prepare the salad: heat the olive oil and butter in a heavy pan.

4 Add the ginger, garlic, chillies and spring onions, cook until the mixture begins to colour, then add the watercress. When it begins to wilt, toss in the lemon juice and season well with salt and pepper.

5 Transfer to a serving dish. Slice the tuna steaks and arrange on top of the salad. Serve the tuna steaks immediately, together with lemon wedges for squeezing over.

Nutritional information per portion: Energy 428kcal/1788kJ; Protein 48g; Carbohydrate 2g, of which sugars 2g; Fat 25g, of which saturates 5g; Cholesterol 56mg; Calcium 58mg; Fibre 0g; Sodium 101mg.

Mackerel in lemon samfaina

Samfaina is a sauce from the east coast of Spain and the Costa Brava. It shares the same ingredients as ratatouille and is rather like a chunky vegetable stew.

SERVES 4

2 large mackerel, filleted, or 4 fillets
plain (all-purpose) flour, for dusting
30ml/2 tbsp olive oil
lemon wedges, if serving cold

FOR THE SAMFAINA SAUCE
1 large aubergine (eggplant)
60ml/4 tbsp olive oil
1 large onion, chopped
2 garlic cloves, finely chopped
1 large courgette (zucchini), sliced
1 red and 1 green (bell) pepper, seeded
    and cut into squares
800g/1¾lb ripe tomatoes, chopped
1 bay leaf
salt and ground black pepper

1 Make the sauce. Peel the aubergine, then cut the flesh into cubes, sprinkle with salt and leave in a colander for 30 minutes.

2 Heat half the oil in a flameproof casserole large enough to fit the fish. Fry the onion over a medium heat until it colours. Add the garlic, then the courgettes and peppers and stir-fry.

3 Add the tomatoes and bay leaf, partially cover and simmer over a low heat, letting the tomatoes just soften without losing their shape.

4 Rinse the aubergine and squeeze dry. Heat the remaining oil in a frying pan. Add the aubergine cubes, and cook, stirring, over a high heat until brown on all sides. Stir into the tomato sauce.

5 Cut each fillet into three, and dust the filleted side with flour. Heat the oil in a frying pan over a high heat and add the fish, floured side down. Fry for 3 minutes until golden. Turn and cook for another minute, then slip the fish into the sauce and simmer, covered, for 5 minutes. Adjust the seasonings, then serve.

Nutritional information per portion: Energy 621kcal/2591kJ; Protein 34.3g; Carbohydrate 32.4g, of which sugars 29.4g; Fat 40.6g, of which saturates 7.6g; Cholesterol 66mg; Calcium 134mg; Fibre 19.4g; Sodium 111mg.

Stuffed sardines

This delicious Tuscan recipe for fresh sardines relies heavily on the fish being freshly caught. Like many recipes from this region, portions are generous, and call for about ten fish per person.

SERVES 4

2–3 stale white bread rolls, crusts
    removed
about 120ml/4fl oz/¹⁄₂ cup milk
40 fresh sardines or large anchovies,
    scaled and filleted
3 eggs, beaten
45ml/3 tbsp grated Parmesan cheese
2 garlic cloves, chopped
a handful of flat leaf parsley, chopped
1 dried red chilli
90ml/6 tbsp plain (all purpose) flour
about 2 litres/3¹⁄₂ pints/9 cups
    sunflower oil, for deep-frying
sea salt

1 Soak the bread in the milk to cover, then squeeze dry. Use any damaged fish fillets for the filling. Put all the perfectly shaped fillets to one side.

2 Mix the bread with the damaged fish, half the beaten eggs, the grated Parmesan cheese, garlic, parsley, chilli and a pinch of salt. Blend it all together with your hands or a fork to make a firm paste.

3 Sandwich two fillets together with a generous spoonful of the filling in the middle, then gently coat first in the remaining beaten egg and then in the flour. Repeat for the pairs of remaining fillets.

4 Heat the oil in large pan until sizzling, then fry the fish, in batches, until crisp and golden brown; about 2 minutes. Drain on kitchen paper and serve.

Nutritional information per portion: Energy 621kcal/2594kJ; Protein 35.8g; Carbohydrate 37.2g, of which sugars 2.6g; Fat 37.7g, of which saturates 9.3g; Cholesterol 155mg; Calcium 343mg; Fibre 1.3g; Sodium 505mg.

Fried salt herring with red onion compote

Salting herring is a classic Scandinavian method of preserving the glut of seasonal fish through the long winter months. This is a great way of perking them up.

SERVES 4

8 salted herring fillets (about 675g/1½ lb total weight)
15g/3oz/1½ cup fine breadcrumbs
40g/1½ oz/3 tbsp butter
2.5ml/½ tsp white pepper

FOR THE RED ONION COMPOTE
675g/1½ lb red onions, diced
75ml/2½ fl oz/⅓ cup cider vinegar
350ml/12fl oz/1½ cups red wine
250ml/8fl oz/1 cup water
50ml/2fl oz/¼ cup honey
15ml/1 tbsp soft light brown sugar
10ml/2 tsp butter
salt and ground black pepper

1 Rinse the herring well in cold water. Place in a bowl of cold water, cover and leave to soak overnight in the refrigerator. Taste the herring for saltiness. If it is too salty, rinse the fillets again. Or, drain, pat dry with kitchen paper and place on a plate.

2 To make the compote, place the onion in a pan and add the vinegar and red wine. Bring to the boil and cook, uncovered, over a medium heat for 30 minutes, stirring often, until the liquid has evaporated.

3 Stir in the water, honey, brown sugar and butter, and season with salt and pepper.

4 Cook the compote for 15 minutes more until reduced and thick. Cover and keep warm until needed.

5 Place the breadcrumbs in a dish and dip the herring fillets into the crumbs to coat both sides. Sprinkle with pepper. Melt the butter in a frying pan over a medium heat.

6 Fry the herring fillets, in batches, turning once, for 4 minutes on each side, until the coating is golden and the fish is cooked. Remove from the pan, drain on kitchen paper, and keep warm until all the fillets are cooked. Spoon the compote over the fish, then serve.

Nutritional information per portion: Energy 672kcal/2805kJ; Protein 35.9g; Carbohydrate 43.5g, of which sugars 23.7g; Fat 34.1g, of which saturates 12.3g; Cholesterol 114mg; Calcium 186mg; Fibre 2.8g; Sodium 460mg.

Fried eel with potatoes in cream sauce

Fried eel is a delicacy in Denmark. Served with boiled or creamed potatoes and accompanied by glasses of icy aquavit and beer, this seasonal dish is a summer speciality.

SERVES 4

1kg/2¼lb eel, skinned and cleaned
1 egg
5ml/1 tsp water
25g/1oz/½ cup breadcrumbs, toasted
10ml/2 tsp salt
2.5ml/½ tsp white pepper
40g/1½ oz/3 tbsp butter
2 lemons, sliced into wedges, to garnish

FOR THE POTATOES

800g/1¾lb potatoes, peeled
5ml/1 tsp salt
40g/1½ oz/3 tbsp butter
20g/¾oz/3 tbsp plain (all-purpose) flour
475ml/16fl oz/2 cups single (light) cream
salt and white pepper, to taste
45ml/3 tbsp fresh parsley, to garnish

1 Cut the eel into 10cm/4in lengths. Whisk together the egg and water in a shallow dish. Place the breadcrumbs in a second dish. Dip the eel into the egg mixture, then into the breadcrumbs to coat both sides. Sprinkle with salt and pepper. Leave to rest for at least 10 minutes.

2 Melt the butter in a large pan over a medium-high heat. Add the eel pieces and cook, turning once, for about 10 minutes on each side.

3 Remove the eel from the pan and drain on kitchen paper. Keep warm.Boil the potatoes in salted water for about 20 minutes. Drain, slice and keep warm.

4 Melt the butter in a pan and stir in the flour. Stir for 5 minutes until the roux is pale beige. Slowly add the cream and cook, stirring, until the sauce has thickened. Season. Stir the potato slices into the cream sauce. Serve with the eel.

Nutritional information per portion: Energy 978kcal/4074kJ; Protein 50.2g; Carbohydrate 43.7g, of which sugars 5.6g; Fat 68.2g, of which saturates 32.3g; Cholesterol 483mg; Calcium 184mg; Fibre 2.3g; Sodium 448mg.

Fish moolie

This is a very popular South-east Asian fish curry in a coconut sauce, which is truly delicious. Choose a firm-textured fish so that the pieces stay intact during the brief cooking process. Monkfish, halibut or cod work well in this dish.

SERVES 4

500g/1¼lb monkfish or other firm-textured fish fillets, skinned and cut into 2.5cm/1in cubes

2.5ml/½ tsp salt

50g/2oz/⅔ cup desiccated (dry unsweetened shredded) coconut

6 shallots, chopped

6 blanched almonds

2–3 garlic cloves, roughly chopped

2.5cm/1in piece fresh root ginger, peeled and sliced

2 lemon grass stalks, trimmed

10ml/2 tsp ground turmeric

45ml/3 tbsp vegetable oil

2 x 400ml/14fl oz cans coconut milk

1–3 fresh red chillies, seeded and sliced into rings

salt and ground black pepper

fresh chives, to garnish

plain boiled or steamed basmati rice, to serve

1 Put the fish cubes in a shallow dish and sprinkle with the salt. Dry-fry the coconut in a wok, turning all the time until it is crisp and golden, then transfer to a food processor and process to an oily paste. Scrape into a bowl and reserve.

2 Add the shallots, almonds, garlic and ginger to the food processor. Chop the bulbous part of each lemon grass stalk and add to the processor with the turmeric. Process the mixture to a paste. Bruise the remaining lemon grass stalks.

3 Heat the oil in a wok. Cook the shallot and spice mixture for about 2–3 minutes. Stir in the coconut milk and bring to the boil, stirring. Add the fish, most of the chilli and the lemon grass stalks. Cook for 3–4 minutes. Stir in the coconut paste and cook for a further 2–3 minutes only. Taste and adjust the seasoning if necessary.

4 Remove the lemon grass. Transfer the moolie to a hot serving dish and sprinkle with the remaining slices of chilli. Garnish with chopped and whole chives and serve with rice.

Nutritional information per portion: Energy 319kcal/1335kJ; Protein 22.4g; Carbohydrate 16.7g, of which sugars 14.9g; Fat 18.6g, of which saturates 8.3g; Cholesterol 18mg; Calcium 96mg; Fibre 3g; Sodium 249mg.

Carp with horseradish sauce

The mighty carp is a traditional fish on Polish menus, where it has been kept for food since the 13th century. There are several varieties, the most flavoursome being the mirror or king carp.

SERVES 4

750ml/1¼ pints/3 cups cold water
120ml/4fl oz/½ cup vinegar
1 medium carp, about 400g/14oz, cut into
    4 fillets
115g/4oz/1 cup plain (all-purpose) flour
115g/4oz/½ cup butter
250ml/8fl oz/1 cup dry white wine
30ml/2 tbsp grated fresh horseradish
2 egg yolks, beaten
30ml/2 tbsp chopped fresh chives
salt and ground black pepper, to taste

1 Mix the water and vinegar in a bowl, then soak the carp in the liquid for 1 hour. Pat dry on kitchen paper, then coat the fish in flour.

2 Melt the butter in a frying pan over a high heat, add the fish and fry for 3–4 minutes on each side, until golden brown. Add the wine to the pan and season, then cover and simmer for 10–15 minutes.

3 Transfer the fish to a serving dish and keep warm.

4 Add the horseradish and egg yolks to the juices in the pan and simmer for 5 minutes, or until thickened.

5 Pour the sauce over the warm fish and garnish with chopped chives. Serve immediately.

Nutritional information per portion: Energy 500kcal/2083kJ; Protein 22.3g; Carbohydrate 23.2g, of which sugars 1.3g; Fat 31.6g, of which saturates 16.7g; Cholesterol 229mg; Calcium 135mg; Fibre 1.5g; Sodium

Salmon with whisky and cream

This Scottish dish combines two of the finest flavours of the country – salmon and whisky. It takes very little time to make, so cook it at the last moment. Serve quite simply.

SERVES 4

4 thin pieces of salmon fillet, about 175g/6oz each

5ml/1 tsp chopped fresh thyme leaves

50g/2oz/¼ cup butter

75ml/5 tbsp whisky

150ml/¼ pint/⅔ cup double (heavy) cream

juice of ½ lemon (optional)

salt and ground black pepper

fresh dill sprigs, to garnish

new potatoes and green beans, to serve

1 Season the salmon with salt, pepper and thyme. Melt the butter in a frying pan. When the butter is foaming, fry the salmon for 2–3 minutes on each side, until they are golden on the outside.

2 Pour 30ml/2 tbsp of the whisky in to the pan, and ignite it. When the flames have died down, carefully transfer the salmon to a plate and keep it hot.

3 Pour the cream into the pan and bring to the boil, stirring and scraping up the cooking juices from the base of the pan. Allow to bubble until reduced and slightly thickened. Season and add the last of the whisky and a squeeze of lemon.

4 Place the salmon on warmed plates, pour the sauce over and garnish with dill. Serve with new potatoes and green beans.

Nutritional information per portion: Energy 637kcal/2637kJ; Protein 36g; Carbohydrate 1g, of which sugars 1g; Fat 50g, of which saturates 22g; Cholesterol 166mg; Calcium 61mg; Fibre 0g; Sodium 163mg.

Fried fish with tartare sauce

Deep-fried pieces of fish – usually perch or pike – is a favourite in Russian restaurants and homes. It is almost always served with a piquant tartare sauce, which is very easy to make.

SERVES 4

700g/1lb 10oz perch fillet, skinned and
    boned
5ml/1 tsp salt
15ml/1 tbsp fresh lemon juice
115g/4oz/1 cup plain (all-purpose) flour
150ml/¼ pint/²/₃ cup light beer
1 egg white
about 1 litre/1¾ pints/4 cups rapeseed
    (canola) oil
lemon wedges, to garnish
green salad, to serve

FOR THE TARTARE SAUCE

3 large pickled gherkins
200g/7fl oz/scant 1 cup mayonnaise
15ml/1 tbsp capers
5ml/1 tsp finely chopped fresh dill
15ml/1 tbsp finely chopped fresh parsley
2.5ml/½ tsp mustard
1.5ml/¼ tsp salt
1.5ml/¼ tsp black pepper

1 To make the tartare sauce, peel and finely chop the gerkins. Put in a bowl with the mayonnaise, capers, dill, parsley and mustard. Mix together. Add salt and pepper to taste, and transfer to a serving bowl.

2 Cut the fish fillets into large chunks and put on a plate. Sprinkle the fish pieces with the salt and lemon juice.

3 Put the flour and beer in a bowl and whisk together until it forms a smooth batter.

4 In a separate bowl, whisk the egg white until it stands in soft peaks, then fold into the batter.

5 Heat the oil in a deep fryer to 180°C/350°F or until a cube of bread browns in 1 minute. Dip and turn the fish pieces in the batter and then drop into the hot oil. Fry for 1–2 minutes, until golden. Using a slotted spoon, remove from the pan and drain on kitchen paper.

6 Serve the fish hot with lemon wedges and the tartare sauce.

Nutritional information per portion: Energy 719kcal/2986kJ; Protein 36.7g; Carbohydrate 24.3g, of which sugars 2.1g; Fat 53.4g, of which saturates 7.6g; Cholesterol 118mg; Calcium 95mg; Fibre 1.8g; Sodium 352mg.

Herb and chilli seared scallops

Tender, succulent scallops are wonderful marinated in fresh chilli, fragrant mint and aromatic basil, then quickly seared. If you can't find king scallops, use twice the quantity of queen scallops.

SERVES 4

20–24 king scallops, cleaned
120ml/4fl oz/½ cup olive oil
finely grated zest and juice of 1 lemon
30ml/2 tbsp finely chopped mixed mint
 and basil
1 red chilli, seeded and finely chopped
salt and ground black pepper
500g/1¼lb pak choi (bok choy),
 separated into leaves

1 Place the scallops in a shallow, dish in a single layer. In a clean bowl, mix together half the oil, the lemon zest and juice, chopped herbs and chilli, and spoon over the scallops. Season well with salt and black pepper, cover and set aside.

2 Heat a wok over a high heat. Drain the scallops (reserving the marinade) and add to the wok. Cook for about 1 minute on each side, or until cooked to your liking.

3 Pour the marinade over the scallops and remove the wok from the heat. Transfer the scallops and juices to a platter and keep warm.

4 Wipe the wok clean and place over a high heat. Add the remaining oil and the pak choi. Stir-fry over a high heat for 2–3 minutes, until the leaves are wilted. Divide the greens among four warmed serving plates, then top with the reserved scallops and their juices and serve.

Nutritional information per portion: Energy 410kcal/1714kJ; Protein 44.5g; Carbohydrate 8.3g, of which sugars 2.1g; Fat 22.3g, of which saturates 3.5g; Cholesterol 82mg; Calcium 286mg; Fibre 3.2g; Sodium 494mg.

Scallops with black pudding and mash

This recipe is a modern twist on a classic Estonian recipe using sweet and delicate scallops, topped with black pudding and nestled on a sweet–savoury mash. Estonians love black pudding and the flavour combinations used here contrast well.

SERVES 4

400g/14oz good-quality, soft black pudding
   (blood sausage), chopped
extra virgin olive oil, for greasing
12 large scallops
salt and ground black pepper
chopped fresh chervil, to garnish
juice of 1 lemon, to serve

FOR THE MASH

4–5 celery sticks, chopped into small pieces
400g/14oz potatoes, peeled and diced
1 large cooking apple, peeled and diced
a pinch of freshly grated nutmeg
knob (pat) of butter (optional)

1 To make the mash, put the celery, potato and apple in a pan and cover with water. Bring to the boil and cook until soft. Drain and mash, or pass through a potato ricer. Season, and add a touch of nutmeg and some butter. You need a firm mash so that it will stay in shape when serving. Keep warm.

2 Preheat the oven to 160°C/325°F/Gas 3. Put the black pudding in a roasting pan and roast for 10–12 minutes. Remove and keep warm.

3 Add a smear of oil to a heavy non-stick frying pan or griddle and heat over high heat. Cook the scallops for about 2 minutes on each side, or until golden brown.

4 To serve, make three small heaps of mash, about 45ml/3 tbsp each, on each serving plate, about 5cm/2in apart. Put a scallop on top of each heap, then top with a small pile of the cooked black pudding. Sprinkle with fresh chervil and squeeze a little lemon juice over the top. Season and serve.

Nutritional information per portion: Energy 457kcal/1916kJ; Protein 26.8g; Carbohydrate 38.5g, of which sugars 5.2g; Fat 22.8g, of which saturates 8.9g; Cholesterol 97mg; Calcium 161mg; Fibre 2.2g; Sodium 1087mg.

Light and fragrant tiger prawns

This simple, elegant dish has a fresh flavour and is suitable both for a simple supper or a dinner party. The delicate flavour of fresh prawns goes well with cucumber and fragrant dill.

SERVES 4

500g/1¼lb raw tiger prawns (jumbo shrimp), peeled, with tail on
500g/1¼lb cucumber
30ml/2 tbsp butter
15ml/1 tbsp olive oil
15ml/1 tbsp finely chopped garlic
45ml/3 tbsp chopped fresh dill
juice of 1 lemon
salt and ground black pepper
steamed rice or noodles, to serve

COOK'S TIP
The best rice to use is jasmine, also known as Thai fragrant rice.

1 With a sharp knife, carefully make a shallow slit along the back of each prawn and use the point of the knife to remove the black vein. Set aside.

2 Peel the cucumber and slice in half lengthways. Using a teaspoon, scoop out all the seeds and discard. Cut the cucumber into sticks.

3 Heat a wok over a high heat, add the butter and oil, and fry the garlic and cucumber for 2–3 minutes.

4 Add the prepared prawns to the wok and continue to stir-fry over a high heat for 3–4 minutes, or until the prawns turn pink and are just cooked through, then remove from the heat.

5 Add the fresh dill and lemon juice to the wok and toss to combine. Season well with salt and ground black pepper and serve immediately, accompanied by steamed rice or noodles.

Nutritional information per portion: Energy 192kcal/798kJ; Protein 23.2g; Carbohydrate 2.5g, of which sugars 1.9g; Fat 9.8g, of which saturates 4.4g; Cholesterol 260mg; Calcium 123mg; Fibre 0.9g; Sodium 287mg.

Baltic fish croquettes

The people of the Baltic States love croquettes, usually using any fish in season, ideally a mixture of smoked and unsmoked. Cold potato salad and gherkins are great accompaniments.

SERVES 4

900g/2lb white fish fillet (smoked or preferably a combination of smoked and unsmoked), bones and skin removed

60ml/4 tbsp white breadcrumbs, plus 75ml/5 tbsp for coating

100ml/3½fl oz/scant ½ cup milk

75–90ml/5–6 tbsp vegetable oil

1 large onion, thinly sliced

2 eggs, beaten

100ml/3½fl oz/scant ½ cup sour cream

15ml/1 tbsp finely chopped fresh marjoram

15ml/1 tbsp creamed horseradish

2 eggs, beaten, for coating

75ml/5 tbsp plain (all purpose) flour, for coating

salt and ground black pepper

1 Chop the fish very finely or pulse it in a food processor, but don't purée it. Transfer to a large bowl.

2 Put the breadcrumbs and milk into a small bowl to soak, then squeeze the breadcrumbs dry, and discard the excess milk. Add the breadcrumbs to the fish.

3 Heat 15ml/1 tbsp oil in a frying pan over a medium heat and add the onion. Cook for 3–4 minutes, or until soft but not browned. Add to the fish mixture.

4 Add the eggs, sour cream, marjoram and horseradish to the fish. Season and mix together. Shape the mixture into croquettes.

5 Coat the croquettes in flour, then in the beaten egg and then in the breadcrumbs. Chill for 30 minutes.

6 Heat the remaining oil in a large non-stick frying pan over a medium heat, and add the fish croquettes in batches, cooking evenly on all sides for 10–12 minutes, or until golden brown and crispy. Serve hot.

Nutritional information per portion: Energy 402kcal/1684kJ; Protein 28.1g; Carbohydrate 33.2g, of which sugars 3.3g; Fat 18.3g, of which saturates 3g; Cholesterol 148mg; Calcium 79mg; Fibre 1.8g; Sodium 622mg.

Mini saffron fishcakes with sweet cucumber

This scented cucumber salad makes a refreshing accompaniment for the fishcakes. Both the fishcakes and salad include the sweet and spicy flavours that are popular in Moroccan food.

SERVES 4

450g/1lb white fish fillets, skinned and cut into chunks
10ml/2 tsp harissa
rind of ½ preserved lemon, finely chopped
bunch of coriander (cilantro), chopped
1 egg
5ml/1 tsp honey
pinch of saffron threads, soaked in 5ml/ 1 tsp water
sunflower oil, for frying
salt and ground black pepper

FOR THE SALAD
2 cucumbers, peeled and grated
juice of 1 orange
juice of ½ lemon
15–30ml/1–2 tbsp orange flower water
15–20ml/3–4 tsp sugar
2.5ml/½ tsp ground cinnamon

1 Make the salad in advance to allow time to chill. Place the cucumber in a strainer over a bowl and sprinkle with some salt. Leave to drain for about 10 minutes. Using your hands, squeeze out the water and place the cucumber in a bowl.

2 In a small jug (pitcher), combine the orange and lemon juice, orange flower water and sugar, and pour over the cucumber. Toss well, sprinkle with cinnamon and chill for at least 1 hour.

3 To make the fishcakes, put the fish in a food processor.

4 Add the harissa, preserved lemon, coriander, egg, honey, saffron with its soaking water, and seasoning to the processor, and process until smooth. Divide into 16 portions. Using wet hands to prevent sticking, roll each portion into a ball and flatten in the palm of your hand.

5 Heat the oil and fry the fishcakes in batches, until golden brown on each side.

6 Drain the fishcakes on kitchen paper and keep hot until they are all cooked. Serve hot, with the cucumber salad.

Nutritional information per portion: Energy 284kcal/1181kJ; Protein 25g; Carbohydrate 10g, of which sugars 10g; Fat 16g, of which saturates 2g; Cholesterol 148mg; Calcium 200mg; Fibre 1g; Sodium 107mg.

Calabrian fish, cheese and chilli patties

This version of fishcakes comes from Southern Italy and is hot and spicy. The fish traditionally used is stockfish, which is dried, and then salted, but another type of salt fish could be used.

SERVES 4–6

1kg/2¼lb stockfish, preferably Stocco di Mammola, soaked in water overnight or until soft
115g/4oz/2 cups soft white breadcrumbs
75g/3oz hard goat's cheese, grated
45ml/3 tbsp chopped fresh flat leaf parsley
1 dried red chilli, chopped
3 garlic cloves, finely chopped
2 eggs, beaten
60ml/4 tbsp olive oil
400g/14oz can chopped tomatoes
sea salt

1 Drain the soaked stockfish, clean and trim it, then flake and chop it finely, removing any bones. Put the fish in a large bowl.

2 Add the breadcrumbs, cheese, parsley, chilli and half the garlic to the bowl. Stir in enough beaten egg to bind the mixture, so it is firm enough to shape the patties. Shaping the patties is easier if the mixture is lightly chilled, so if there is time, put it into the refrigerator for 30 minutes.

3 Divide the mixture into 8–12 portions and shape into patties. Set aside. Heat the olive oil in a large frying pan and add the remaining garlic. Fry over gentle heat for about 3 minutes. As soon as the garlic begins to brown, stir in the canned tomatoes. Simmer the sauce for about 10 minutes.

4 Add the stockfish patties and spoon the sauce over to coat. Cover and simmer for 10–15 minutes until cooked, then serve.

Nutritional information per portion: Energy 346kcal/1450kJ; Protein 38.2g; Carbohydrate 17.3g, of which sugars 2.9g; Fat 14.2g, of which saturates 4g; Cholesterol 152mg; Calcium 87mg; Fibre 1.5g; Sodium 353mg.

Cinnamon fishcakes with currants

Whether served as an appetizer or as a main course with a salad, these fresh, tasty fishcakes are delicious, flavoured with cinnamon and a triad of herbs – parsley, mint and dill.

SERVES 4

450g/1lb skinless fresh white fish fillets, such as haddock or sea bass

2 slices of day-old bread, sprinkled with water, left for a few minutes, then squeezed dry

1 red onion, finely chopped

30ml/2 tbsp currants, soaked in warm water for 5–10 minutes and drained

30ml/2 tbsp pine nuts

1 bunch each of fresh flat leaf parsley, mint and dill, chopped

1 egg

5–10ml/1–2 tsp tomato purée (paste)

15ml/1 tbsp ground cinnamon

45–60ml/3–4 tbsp plain (all-purpose) flour

45–60ml/3–4 tbsp sunflower oil

salt and ground black pepper

salad leaves and 1–2 lemons or limes, cut into wedges, to serve

1 In a bowl, break up the fish with a fork. Add the bread, onion, currants and pine nuts, toss in the herbs and mix well.

2 In another small bowl, beat the egg with the tomato purée and 10ml/2 tsp of the cinnamon. Pour the mixture over the fish.

3 Season with salt and pepper, then mix with your hands and mould into small balls.

4 Mix the flour on a plate with the remaining cinnamon. Press each ball into a flat cake and coat in the flour.

5 Heat the oil in a wide, shallow pan and fry the fishcakes in batches for 8–10 minutes, until golden brown. Lift out and drain on kitchen paper. Serve hot on a bed of leaves, with lemon or lime wedges for squeezing.

Nutritional information per portion: Energy 317kcal/1324kJ; Protein 26.1g; Carbohydrate 17.8g, of which sugars 2.5g; Fat 16.2g, of which saturates 1.9g; Cholesterol 99mg; Calcium 79mg; Fibre 1.6g; Sodium 169mg.

Trout burgers

These tasty home-made tasty fish burgers really are a treat. They also provide the ideal way of persuading children who claim they don't like fish to try it.

MAKES 8

350g/12oz trout fillet, skinned
150ml/½ pint/⅔ cup milk
150ml/¼ pint/⅔ cup hot fish stock
4 spring onions (scallions), thinly sliced
350g/12oz cooked potatoes, peeled
5ml/1 tsp tartare sauce
1 egg, beaten
50g/2oz/1 cup fresh white breadcrumbs
60ml/4 tbsp semolina
salt and ground white pepper
vegetable oil, for shallow-frying

TO SERVE

120ml/4fl oz/½ cup mayonnaise
45ml/3 tbsp drained canned corn
1 red (bell) pepper, seeded and finely diced
8 burger buns
4 ripe tomatoes, sliced, and salad leaves

1 Place the trout in a frying pan with the milk, stock and spring onions. Simmer for 5 minutes or until the fish is cooked.

2 Lift the fish out of the pan and set it aside. Strain the stock into a bowl, reserving the spring onions.

3 Mash the potatoes roughly and stir in the tartare sauce, egg and breadcrumbs. Flake the trout and add the reserved spring onions. Fold into the potato mixture and season. Divide into eight portions.

4 Shape each portion into burgers, using your hands. Coat thoroughly in the semolina and pat them into shape. Arrange on a plate and refrigerate for 1 hour, to firm up. In a bowl, mix the mayonnaise with the corn and red pepper.

5 Heat the oil in a frying pan and when hot fry the burgers, on a medium heat, for 3–4 minutes on each side until golden. To serve, split the buns and spread mayonnaise over each half. Add salad leaves, tomato and a burger and serve.

Nutritional information per portion: Energy 461kcal/1936kJ; Protein 18g; Carbohydrate 47g, of which sugars 6g; Fat 23g, of which saturates 4g; Cholesterol 72mg; Calcium 120mg; Fibre 4g; Sodium 484mg.

Haddock with fennel butter

The freshest fish tastes fabulous when cooked in a simple herb butter. Here the aniseed flavour of fennel complements the haddock beautifully to make a simple dish ideal for a dinner party.

SERVES 4

675g/1½ lb haddock fillet, skinned and cut into 4 portions
50g/2oz/¼ cup butter
1 lemon
45ml/3 tbsp coarsely chopped fennel

1 Preheat the oven to 220°C/ 425°F/Gas 7. Season the fish on both sides with salt and pepper. Melt a quarter of the butter in a frying pan, preferably non-stick, and cook the fish over a medium heat briefly on both sides.

2 Transfer the fish to a shallow ovenproof dish. Cut four wafer-thin slices from the lemon and squeeze the juice from the remainder over the fish.

3 Place the lemon slices on top and then bake for 15–20 minutes, or until the fish is cooked.

4 Meanwhile, melt the remaining butter in the frying pan and add the fennel and a little seasoning.

5 Transfer the cooked fish to plates and pour the cooking juices into the herb butter. Heat gently for a few seconds, then pour the herb butter over the fish. Serve immediately.

Nutritional information per portion: Energy 231kcal/970kJ; Protein 32.3g; Carbohydrate 0.3g, of which sugars 0.3g; Fat 11.3g, of which saturates 6.7g; Cholesterol 87mg; Calcium 29mg; Fibre 0.3g; Sodium 190mg.

Pan-fried citrus trout with basil

The clean taste of oranges and lemons and the aromatic scent of basil combine beautifully in this recipe to create a light and tangy sauce for trout fillets.

SERVES 4

4 trout fillets, each about 200g/7oz
2 lemons, 1 with zest grated then
squeezed and 1 sliced
3 oranges, 2 with zest grated then
squeezed and 1 sliced
105ml/7 tbsp olive oil
45ml/3 tbsp plain (all-purpose) flour
25g/1oz/2 tbsp butter
5ml/1 tsp soft light brown sugar
15g/1/2 oz/1/2 cup fresh basil leaves,
shredded
salt and ground black pepper

1 Arrange the trout fillets in a ovenproof dish. Mix the lemon and orange rind and juices into a bowl.

2 Add 75ml/5 tbsp of the oil to the citrus juices. Beat with a fork and pour over the fish. Cover and leave to marinate in the refrigerator for at least 2 hours. Preheat the oven to 150°C/300°F/Gas 2.

3 Remove the trout from the marinade. Season the fish and coat each fillet in flour.

4 Heat the remaining oil in a frying pan and fry the fish for 2–3 minutes on each side. Remove and keep hot.

5 Add the butter and marinade to the pan and heat gently, stirring until the butter melts. Season with salt and pepper, and add the sugar.

6 Cook gently for 4–5 minutes until the sauce has thickened slightly. Add half the basil leaves to the pan. Pour the sauce over the fish and garnish with basil and the citrus slices.

Nutritional information per portion: Energy 266kcal/1119kJ; Protein 40.5g; Carbohydrate 7.9g, of which sugars 7.7g; Fat 8.3g, of which saturates 0.2g; Cholesterol 0mg; Calcium 140mg; Fibre 1.7g; Sodium 177mg.

Pollock with onions

A member of the cod family, pollock is a favourite, less expensive alternative that is often served along the Norwegian coast. The flesh is much firmer than cod and has a slightly pearly hue.

SERVES 4

50g/2oz/½ cup plain (all-purpose) flour
675g/1½ lb thick pollock fillet, skinned
    and cut into 4 serving portions
50g/2oz/4 tbsp butter
15ml/1 tbsp vegetable oil
2 large onions, sliced
5ml/1 tsp sugar
200ml/7fl oz/scant 1 cup water
salt and ground black pepper
boiled potatoes and a green vegetable,
    such as cabbage, to serve

1 Preheat the oven to 180°C/350°F/Gas 4. Put the flour on a large plate and season. Dip the fish in the flour to coat on both sides.

2 Put a knob (pat) of the butter and the oil in a large frying pan and heat until the butter has melted. Add the floured fish and fry quickly on both sides. Place in an ovenproof dish.

3 Melt the remaining butter in the same pan, add the onions, season and fry gently for about 10 minutes until softened and golden brown.

4 Add the sugar, increase the heat and allow the onion to caramelize slightly, stirring.

5 Spread the onions over the fish. Add the water to the frying pan, stirring to lift any sediment on the bottom of the pan, bring to the boil then pour over the fish and onions.

6 Bake in the oven for about 10–15 minutes, until the fish is tender. Serve the pollock with boiled potatoes and a green vegetable, such as cabbage.

Nutritional information per portion: Energy 298kcal/1247kJ; Protein 32.9g; Carbohydrate 16g, of which sugars 5g; Fat 11.8g, of which saturates 6.7g; Cholesterol 104mg; Calcium 52mg; Fibre 1.3g; Sodium 180mg.

Stuffed white fish wrapped in bacon

Plentiful but rather bland fish such as whiting and lemon sole, plaice and flounder, work well in this recipe. Serve with boiled new potatoes and a fresh, green vegetable.

SERVES 4

4 good-size or 8 small fish fillets, such as
    whiting, trimmed
4 streaky (fatty) bacon rashers (strips)

FOR THE STUFFING

50g/2oz/¼ cup butter
1 onion, finely chopped
50g/2oz/1 cup fine fresh brown
    breadcrumbs
5ml/1 tsp finely chopped fresh parsley
a good pinch of mixed dried herbs
sea salt and ground black pepper
new potatoes and green beans or
    broccoli, to serve

1 Preheat the oven to 190°C/375°F/ Gas 5. Cut large fillets of fish in half lengthways. Melt the butter in a small pan, add the onion and cook gently until softened but not browned. Add the breadcrumbs, parsley and herbs. Season to taste.

2 Divide the stuffing between the fillets, roll them up and wrap a bacon rasher around each one.

3 Secure the rolls with wooden cocktail sticks (toothpicks) and place the rolls in a single layer in the base of a shallow buttered ovenproof dish.

4 Cover with foil and bake in the preheated oven for about 15 minutes, removing the cover for the last 5 minutes. Serve the stuffed fish with potatoes and green beans or broccoli.

Nutritional information per portion: Energy 344Kcal/1436kJ; Protein 38.1g; Carbohydrate 12.5g, of which sugars 2.4g; Fat 15.9g, of which saturates 8.2g; Cholesterol 120mg; Calcium 44mg; Fibre 0.8g; Sodium 662mg.

Fish baked with cardamom, cinnamon and cloves

This gently-spiced and succulent fish recipe is cooked by sealing the food into a heavy pan with a tight-fitting lid, so it cooks in the steam and flavour cannot escape.

SERVES 4

675g/1½ lb tilapia or monkfish fillets, or any other firm, white fish, cut into 5cm/2in pieces
15ml/1 tbsp lemon juice
5ml/1 tsp salt
2.5cm/1in piece of cinnamon stick
seeds of 6 green cardamom pods
5ml/1 tsp cumin seeds
10ml/2 tsp coriander seeds
15ml/1 tbsp white poppy seeds
15ml/1 tbsp sesame seeds
60ml/4 tbsp sunflower oil or olive oil
1 large onion, finely chopped
5ml/2 tsp garlic purée
10ml/2 tsp ginger purée
2.5–5ml/½–1 tsp chilli powder
2.5ml/½ tsp ground turmeric
115g/4oz/½ cup thick set natural (plain) yogurt, whisked
2 medium tomatoes, sliced
2–3 tbsp chopped coriander (cilantro) leaves

1 Sprinkle the fish with the lemon juice and half the salt. Set aside for 20 minutes to absorb the flavours. Preheat the oven to 160°C/325°F/Gas Mark 3. Finely grind the cinnamon, cardamom seeds, cumin, coriander, poppy and sesame seeds in a coffee grinder. Set aside.

2 In a small pan, heat the oil over a medium heat and add the onion. Fry until it is soft, but not browned.

3 Add the garlic and ginger to the pan, fry for 2 minutes, then add the ground ingredients, chilli powder and turmeric. Cook for 1 minute, stirring, to release the aromas, then add the remaining salt.

4 Remove the pan of spices from the heat and beat in the yogurt, then set aside.

5 In a roasting pan (15cm x 30cm/6in x 12in), spread half the spice mixture, half the tomatoes and half the chopped coriander.

6 Arrange the fish on top in a single layer. Carefully spread the remaining spice mix, chopped coriander and tomatoes over the fish.

7 Cover the pan with a piece of foil, sealing the edges completely. Bake in the centre of the oven for 35–40 minutes. Transfer to a dish and strain the juices over.

Nutritional information per portion: Energy 353kcal/1473kJ; Protein 36.2g; Carbohydrate 17.8g, of which sugars 10.6g; Fat 15.9g, of which saturates 2.3g; Cholesterol 0.2mg; Calcium 320mg; Fibre 2.2g; Sodium 126mg.

Piran baked fish

The old seaport of Piran lies at the tip of the peninsula on the coastline of Slovenia. This beautiful historic town gives its name to a popular dish served in its many local restaurants.

SERVES 4

675g/1½ lb white fish fillets, such as pike, carp or perch
40g/1½ oz/¼ cup raisins
30ml/2 tbsp lemon juice
30ml/2 tbsp cold water
45ml/3 tbsp olive oil
2 onions, peeled and sliced
2 leeks, thinly sliced
2 garlic cloves, crushed
1 carrot, peeled and diced
115g/4oz green beans, cut into 2.5cm/1in lengths
60ml/4 tbsp chopped fresh dill
salt and ground black pepper
steamed new potatoes, to serve

1 Preheat the oven to 180°C/ 350°F/ Gas 4. Grease an ovenproof dish and arrange the fish fillets in a single layer along the bottom.

2 Put the raisins in a small bowl with the lemon juice and the water. Leave to soak for a few minutes.

3 Heat the olive oil in a frying pan and gently cook the onions and leeks for 5 minutes, until they begin to soften. Stir in the garlic, carrot and green beans and cook for an additional 3–4 minutes.

4 Add the raisins and soaking liquid. Gently heat until they are piping hot. Season with salt and pepper.

5 Spoon the vegetable mixture over the fish and then tightly cover with a piece of foil. Bake in the oven for 20–25 minutes, or until the fish is just tender and the vegetables are cooked.

6 Sprinkle the top of the fish with the chopped dill before serving this dish with some steamed tender new potatoes.

Nutritional information per portion: Energy 373kcal/1564kJ; Protein 33.5g; Carbohydrate 22.5g, of which sugars 19.3g; Fat 17.3g, of which saturates 2.9g; Cholesterol 113mg; Calcium 149mg; Fibre 5.3g; Sodium 97mg.

Hake with turnip tops and onions

This recipe comes from the north of Portugal, where hake is highly prized and served in many different ways. A member of the cod family, hake has a deliciously soft texture and an excellent flavour, but is quite fragile, which is why it is often sold as steaks rather than fillets.

SERVES 4

105ml/7 tbsp olive oil

2 small onions, chopped

2 garlic cloves, chopped

5ml/1 tsp sweet paprika

1 bay leaf

15ml/1 tbsp white wine vinegar

150ml/¼ pint/⅔ cup fish stock or water

4 hake steaks, about 225g/8oz each

200g/7oz turnip tops (the green part of the turnip)

8 potatoes, boiled without peeling

4 hard-boiled eggs, halved

salt

1 Preheat the oven to 180°C/350°F/Gas 4. Heat 30ml/2 tbsp of the olive oil in a flameproof casserole. Add the onions, garlic, paprika and bay leaf and cook over a low heat, stirring occasionally, for 5 minutes, until the onions have softened.

2 Add the vinegar and the stock or water, then place the hake in the casserole and season with salt. Cover and cook in the oven for 15 minutes.

3 Meanwhile, steam the turnip tops or cook in a little boiling water for 3–5 minutes, then drain if necessary. Press them through a sieve (strainer) into a bowl, mix with 15ml/1 tbsp of the remaining olive oil and keep warm.

4 Peel the potatoes and cut into quarters. Heat the remaining olive oil in a sauté pan or frying pan, add the potatoes and cook over a medium-low heat, turning occasionally, for 7–8 minutes until light golden brown.

5 Using a fish slice or slotted spoon, transfer the fish to a large serving plate. Add the potatoes, turnip tops and eggs and spoon over the onion sauce to serve.

Nutritional information per portion: Energy 614kcal/2571kJ; Protein 51g; Carbohydrate 36.2g, of which sugars 5.7g; Fat 30.7g, of which saturates 5.2g; Cholesterol 242mg; Calcium 102mg; Fibre 3.4g; Sodium 326mg.

Roasted sea bream

This is a classic way of cooking a whole fish. The sauce is juicy and combines superbly with the taste of the bream. You can also roast individual portions using the same method.

SERVES 4

1 red bream or porgy, weighing 1.6–2kg/3½–4½ lb, scaled and cleaned
105ml/7 tbsp olive oil
2 onions, sliced
2 garlic cloves, chopped
2 bay leaves
2 ripe tomatoes, peeled and diced
50ml/2fl oz/¼ cup white wine
sea salt
chopped fresh parsley, to garnish
potatoes and vegetables, to serve

1 Preheat the oven to 180°C/ 350°F/Gas 4. Using a sharp knife, slash the fish twice on each side. Place it in a large, shallow ovenproof dish or roasting pan, drizzle with 60ml/4 tbsp of the olive oil and sprinkle with salt. Place in the oven and roast for about 10 minutes, until the fish is half cooked.

2 Heat the remaining oil in a frying pan. Add the sliced onions, garlic and bay leaves and cook over a low heat, stirring occasionally, for 5 minutes, until soft and translucent.

3 Add the diced tomatoes and the white wine to the pan. Bring to the boil then simmer gently to warm the sauce through.

4 When the fish has been in the oven for about 10 minutes, spoon the onion mixture over it, return to the oven and roast for a further 10 minutes until tender.

5 Transfer to a serving dish, sprinkle with the parsley and serve immediately with cooked potatoes and vegetables.

Nutritional information per portion: Energy 403kcal/1679kJ; Protein 32.5g; Carbohydrate 11.5g, of which sugars 8.6g; Fat 24.7g, of which saturates 2.8g; Cholesterol 67mg; Calcium 106mg; Fibre 2.3g; Sodium 201mg.

Crusted garlic and parsley monkfish

Monkfish is a lovely juicy fish that was once sold as 'scampi' because its firm texture was not fashionable. Now it is considered a prime fish that needs simple cooking.

SERVES 4

4 monkfish tails, slashed diagonally two or three times
115g/4oz/generous 1 cup dried breadcrumbs
salt and ground black pepper

FOR THE GARLIC BUTTER
115g/4oz/½ cup softened butter
2 cloves finely chopped garlic
15ml/1 tbsp finely chopped parsley

1 Preheat the oven to 220°C/425°F/Gas 7. First make the garlic butter, mix the butter, garlic and parsley together in a small bowl.

2 Season the fish with salt and freshly ground black pepper. Using your fingertips, rub the garlic butter liberally all over, ensuring that you have pushed a good quantity into each of the diagonal slashes.

3 Sprinkle the breadcrumbs over the fish, place on a baking tray and bake for 10–15 minutes.

4 Check the fish is cooked – the tails should be golden brown, with white slashes where the cuts have opened up to reveal the succulent flesh inside. Serve at once, with any juices in the pan.

Nutritional information per portion: Energy 272kcal/1130kJ; Protein 11.4g; Carbohydrate 9.9g, of which sugars 0.5g; Fat 21.1g, of which saturates 13.1g; Cholesterol 62mg; Calcium 26mg; Fibre 0.3g; Sodium 258mg.

Monkfish with rocket pesto

An intensely-flavoured topping complements the rich monkfish in this recipe. As it cooks, monkfish tends to give off milky juices, which can have the effect of boiling the fish. One way to counteract this is to season with salt and leave for an hour to draw out excess moisture.

SERVES 4

900g/2lb monkfish tail fillets, salted and left to
    stand for 1 hour
50g/2oz rocket (arugula)
30ml/2 tbsp pine nuts
1 garlic clove, chopped
25g/1oz/1/3 cup freshly grated Parmesan cheese
90ml/6 tbsp olive oil

45ml/3 tbsp lemon juice
2 red (bell) peppers, halved
2 yellow (bell) peppers, halved
1 red onion, cut into wedges
2 courgettes (zucchini), sliced
4 fresh rosemary sprigs
salt and ground black pepper

1 Rinse the salted fish and pat dry. Set aside. Preheat the oven to 220°C/425°F/Gas 7. Place the rocket, pine nuts, garlic, Parmesan cheese, 45ml/3 tbsp of the olive oil and 15ml/1 tbsp of the lemon juice in a food processor or blender and process to a smooth paste.

2 Lay one fish fillet out flat, cut-side up and spread with the pesto. Place the remaining fillet on top, cut-side down. Tie the fish with string at intervals to seal together. Sprinkle with plenty of salt and pepper to season and set aside. Cut each pepper half into three lengthways. Remove the core and seeds.

3 Place the pepper in an ovenproof casserole with the onion wedges and slices of courgette. In a small bowl, mix 15ml/1 tbsp of the olive oil and the remaining lemon juice. Add to the vegetables. Season with salt and pepper.

4 Tuck the rosemary sprigs among the vegetables. Cover the casserole, place in the oven and cook the vegetables for 20 minutes. Place the monkfish parcel in the centre of the vegetables and brush it with 15ml/1 tbsp of the olive oil. Sprinkle the remaining oil over the vegetables.

5 Cover again and return the pan to the oven until the monkfish is cooked through and turns opaque. To serve, cut the fish into thick slices, removing the string, if you prefer, and serve with the cooked vegetables.

Nutritional information per portion: Energy 477Kcal/1991kJ; Protein 47g; Carbohydrate 14.7g, of which sugars 13.7g; Fat 25.8g, of which saturates 4.5g; Cholesterol 42mg; Calcium 160mg; Fibre 4.3g; Sodium 139mg.

Sea bass baked in salt

This ancient Mediterranean method of cooking a whole fish intensifies its freshness, conjuring up the taste of the sea. Little accompaniment is needed; serve with lemon and a tomato salad.

SERVES 2–4

1.2kg/2½ lb very fresh sea bass, gutted, with head and tail left on
about 1kg/2¼lb coarse sea salt
ground black pepper and lemon wedges, to serve

COOK'S TIPS

Most large whole fish can be cooked this way. Use the cheapest coarse salt you can find, you don't want to waste premium sea salt on this recipe.

1 Preheat the oven to 190°C/375°F/ Gas 5. Rinse the fish inside and out. Find an ovenproof dish to fit the fish and cover the bottom with a thick layer of salt, pressing it down with the heel of your hand.

2 Place the fish on the salt layer and shovel spoonfuls of salt over it until it is completely covered, then press gently to compact it.

3 Put the dish in the oven and bake for 1 hour, until the salt has formed a hard crust.

4 To serve, crack open the salt crust. Carefully peel off the top layer of salt, removing the skin of the fish with it, and being careful not to dislodge salt on to the flesh. Serve immediately, with black pepper and a squeeze of lemon.

Nutritional information per portion: Energy 175kcal/737kJ; Protein 33.8g; Carbohydrate 0g, of which sugars 0g; Fat 4.4g, of which saturates 0.7g; Cholesterol 140mg; Calcium 228mg; Fibre 0g; Sodium 1103mg.

Fillets of brill in red wine sauce

Forget the old maxim that red wine and fish do not go well together. The robust sauce adds colour and richness to this excellent dish, which is more than elegant enough for a dinner party.

SERVES 4

4 fillets of brill, about 175–200g/6–7oz
    each, skinned
150g/5oz/10 tbsp chilled butter, diced,
    plus extra, for greasing
115g/4oz shallots, thinly sliced
200ml/7fl oz/scant 1 cup red wine
200ml/7fl oz/scant 1 cup fish stock
salt and ground white pepper
fresh flat leaf parsley leaves or chervil,
    to garnish

1 Preheat the oven to 180°C/ 350°F/Gas 4. Season the fish fillets on both sides with salt and ground black pepper. Generously butter a shallow flameproof dish. Spread the shallots in the dish and lay the fish fillets on top. Season generously.

2 Pour in the red wine and fish stock, cover the dish with a lid or foil and then bring the liquid to just below boiling point. Transfer to the oven and bake for 6–8 minutes, or until the brill is just cooked.

3 Lift the fish and shallots on to a serving dish, cover and keep warm. Transfer the dish to the stove and bring the liquid to the boil over a high heat until reduced by half. Lower the heat and whisk in the chilled butter, a piece at a time, to make a smooth, shiny sauce. Set the sauce aside and keep hot.

4 Divide the shallots among warmed plates and lay the brill fillets on top. Pour the sauce over and garnish with parsley or chervil.

Nutritional information per portion: Energy 515Kcal/2142kJ; Protein 35.6g; Carbohydrate 2.6g, of which sugars 1.9g; Fat 36.7g, of which saturates 19.5g; Cholesterol 156mg; Calcium 98mg; Fibre 0.4g; Sodium 452mg.

Baked pike in sour cream

This freshwater fish has lean creamy-white flesh, and needs to be kept moist during cooking. Here it is gently baked in a creamy sauce. Serve with sautéed potatoes.

SERVES 4–6

1.5kg/3lb whole pike
1 bay leaf
15ml/1 tbsp olive oil
50g/2oz/¼ cup butter
1 onion, chopped
1 garlic clove, chopped
115g/4oz/1½ cups wild mushrooms, thickly sliced
15ml/1 tbsp plain (all-purpose) flour
175ml/6fl oz/¾ cup sour cream
15ml/1 tbsp chopped fresh parsley
salt and ground black pepper

COOK'S TIP

Pike is a very bony fish, and even when filleted should be checked for tiny pin bones.

1 Preheat the oven to 190°C/ 375°F/ Gas 5. Clean, skin and fillet the pike, putting the bones and skin into a pan. Pour over just enough cold water to cover and add the bay leaf. Slowly bring to the boil, reduce the heat and gently simmer, uncovered, for 20 minutes, then strain the stock and reserve.

2 Heat the oil and half the butter in a frying pan and cook the onion for 7–8 minutes, until soft. Add the garlic and mushrooms and cook for 2 more minutes.

3 Add 300ml/½ pint/1¼ cups of the stock to the onion mixture and simmer for 5 minutes.

4 Use the remaining butter to grease an ovenproof dish. Arrange the fillets in the dish and season. Blend the flour with the sour cream and pour into the onion mixture. Bring to the boil, stirring, then carefully pour over the fish.

5 Cover the dish with foil and bake for 30 minutes, until the fish is tender. Serve, sprinkled with parsley.

Nutritional information per portion: Energy 310kcal/1299kJ; Protein 40.2g; Carbohydrate 3.1g, of which sugars 1.2g; Fat 15.3g, of which saturates 5.7g; Cholesterol 178mg; Calcium 92mg; Fibre 0.3g; Sodium 158mg.

Oven-roasted carp

This freshwater fish has a firm flesh and is delicious when it is cooked on a base of sliced local new potatoes and caramelized white onions. The bacon helps to seal in the flavour and baste the fish.

SERVES 4

25g/1oz/2 tbsp butter, preferably
 unsalted
500g/1¼lb new potatoes, cut into
 2cm/½in thick slices
15ml/1 tbsp olive oil
1 large onion, thinly sliced
1 garlic clove, crushed
10ml/2 tsp cider vinegar
about 900g/2lb whole carp, cleaned
115g/4oz rindless smoked streaky (fatty)
 bacon rashers (strips)
salt and ground black pepper
steamed green cabbage, to serve

1 Preheat the oven to 180°C/ 350°F/Gas 4. Use half of the butter to grease an ovenproof dish.

2 Bring a large pan of salted water to the boil. Add the potatoes to the water, bring back to the boil and simmer for 10 minutes, until they are almost tender. Remove from the pan and place in the bottom of the prepared dish. Spoon over 60ml/ 4 tbsp of the cooking liquid.

3 Meanwhile, heat the remaining butter and oil in a frying pan and cook the onions for 10 minutes on a medium heat until soft and golden.

4 Add the garlic to the onions and cook for a further 2 minutes until golden. Stir in the cider vinegar.

5 Spoon the onions over the potatoes. Place the carp fillets on top of the onions, then season. Arrange the bacon rashers on top.

6 Cover with foil and bake in the oven for 20 minutes. Remove the foil and bake for a further 15–20 minutes or until the bacon is browned and the fish is tender and flakes easily with a fork. Serve immediately with some steamed green cabbage.

Nutritional information per portion: Energy 438kcal/1836kJ; Protein 41.6g; Carbohydrate 20.1g, of which sugars 1.6g; Fat 21.8g, of which saturates 7.8g; Cholesterol 177mg; Calcium 64mg; Fibre 1.3g; Sodium 554mg.

Baked trout with a gremolata crust

A gremolata crust is a delicious combination of breadcrumbs with finely chopped parsley, lemon rind and garlic. It is traditionally sprinkled over the classic veal dish, osso bucco, but is equally good with fish, as it seals in the moisture and keeps the fish from going dry.

SERVES 4

1 small aubergine (eggplant), diced
1 red (bell) pepper, finely diced
1 yellow (bell) pepper, finely diced
1 small red onion, finely chopped
30ml/2 tbsp olive oil
350g/12oz trout fillets
juice of 1 lime
salt and ground black pepper
chunks of bread, to serve

FOR THE GREMOLATA CRUST

grated rind of 1 lemon
grated rind of 1 lime
25g/1oz/½ cup fresh breadcrumbs
30ml/2 tbsp chopped fresh flat leaf parsley
1 garlic clove, finely chopped

1 Preheat the oven to 200°C/400°F/Gas 6. Place the aubergine, peppers and onion in a roasting pan. Add the oil and stir to coat all the vegetables. Sprinkle with plenty of salt and ground black pepper. Cook for 40 minutes or until the edges of the vegetables have begun to char.

2 Make the gremolata by mixing the lemon and lime rind with the breadcrumbs, parsley and garlic. Add plenty of salt and ground black pepper.

3 Place the trout fillets on top of the vegetables in the roasting pan and cover the surface of the fish with the breadcrumb mixture. Return to the oven for a further 15 minutes or until the fish is fully cooked and the gremolata topping is golden and crunchy.

4 Divide the fish and vegetables among four individual warmed serving plates and sprinkle the lime juice over to taste. Serve with chunks of bread to soak up all the juices.

Nutritional information per portion: Energy 237kcal/992kJ; Protein 20g; Carbohydrate 12g, of which sugars 7g; Fat 13g, of which saturates 2g; Cholesterol 59mg; Calcium 43mg; Fibre 3g; Sodium 92mg.

Stuffed trout with tarragon sauce

Tarragon and trout make a marvellous combination. Here, trout are filled with a herb stuffing before being baked in wine and served with a creamy tarragon sauce.

SERVES 4

90ml/6 tbsp fresh white breadcrumbs

30ml/2 tbsp chopped fresh tarragon

1 egg, beaten

4 whole trout, each about 200g/7oz, cleaned and boned

1 small onion, sliced

150ml/¼ pint/²⁄₃ cup dry white wine

8 fresh tarragon sprigs

25g/1oz/2 tbsp butter

15ml/1 tbsp plain (all-purpose) flour

150ml/¼ pint/²⁄₃ cup single (light) cream

salt and ground black pepper

steamed green vegetables and lime wedges, to serve

1 Preheat the oven to 190°C/375°F/Gas 5. Mix the breadcrumbs with half the tarragon in a bowl. Season, then bind the mixture with the beaten egg. Spread a layer of tarragon stuffing inside the cavity of each trout, pressing the mixture down firmly. Season the trout well.

2 Place the trout in a single layer in a baking dish. Add the onion slices and wine to the dish and top each fish with a sprig of tarragon. Cover with foil. Bake for 20–25 minutes. Remove from the oven and strain the cooking liquid into a measuring jug (cup). Keep the fish warm.

3 Add water to make the stock up to 150ml/¼ pint/²⁄₃ cup of liquid. Melt the butter in a pan, stir in the flour and cook, stirring, for 1–2 minutes. Gradually add the cooking liquid, stirring constantly.

4 Add the cream in the same way and bring to the boil. Continue to stir as the mixture thickens to a smooth sauce. Season and add the remaining tarragon.

5 Remove the skin, heads and tails from the trout and place on warmed plates. Pour over the sauce. Serve with steamed vegetables.

Nutritional information per portion: Energy 462kcal/933kJ; Protein 44g; Carbohydrate 11g, of which sugars 2g; Fat 25g, of which saturates 11g; Cholesterol 226mg; Calcium 108mg; Fibre 1g; Sodium 221mg.

Calabrian baked swordfish

The perfect accompaniment to this delicious swordfish dish is a platter of grilled vegetables. Swordfish is a lovely, meaty fish that goes perfectly with these robust Mediterranean flavours.

SERVES 4

4 thick swordfish steaks, about 175g/
 6oz each
225g/8oz/4 cups soft white breadcrumbs
150g/5oz Pecorino cheese, grated
45ml/3 tbsp flat leaf parsley, chopped
90ml/6 tbsp extra virgin olive oil
juice of 1 lemon, plus wedges to serve
salt and ground black pepper

VARIATIONS
Use tuna steaks instead of swordfish, adjusting the cooking times if necessary. Flavour the breadcrumb topping by adding some chopped olives and rinsed and chopped capers.

1 Rinse and dry the swordfish steaks. Preheat the oven to 180°C/350°F/Gas 4.

2 Put the breadcrumbs in a bowl and add the grated cheese and parsley. Season with salt and pepper to taste and mix well.

3 Use a little of the olive oil to grease a baking dish which is just large enough to hold the steaks snugly in one layer. Brush the steaks with oil on both sides.

4 Spread half the breadcrumb mixture over the base of the dish, and lay the swordfish steaks on top. Season the fish with salt and pepper.

5 Cover with the rest of the breadcrumb mixture, then drizzle with the remaining oil. Bake for 10 minutes, then take the dish out of the oven, pour the lemon juice evenly over the crumb topping and return to the oven for 10 minutes more. Serve hot with grilled vegetables and lemon wedges.

Nutritional information per portion: Energy 737kcal/3089kJ; Protein 57.4g; Carbohydrate 43.9g, of which sugars 1.8g; Fat 38g, of which saturates 11.9g; Cholesterol 118mg; Calcium 557mg; Fibre 1.9g; Sodium 1103mg.

Salmon with Stilton

A rich blue Stilton and herb butter creates a flavoursome sauce for these salmon steaks, which are baked in white wine. Serve this totally mouthwatering mélange with new potatoes, stir-fried red and yellow peppers and mangetouts.

SERVES 4

115g/4oz Stilton cheese

25g/1oz/2 tbsp butter, softened

15ml/1 tbsp chopped fresh chives, plus extra,
   to garnish

15ml/1 tbsp chopped fresh thyme leaves

1 garlic clove, crushed

30ml/2 tbsp olive oil

4 salmon steaks

60ml/4 tbsp dry white wine

salt and ground black pepper

new potatoes, stir-fried red and yellow (bell) peppers and
   mangetouts (snow peas), to serve

1 Crumble the Stilton and place it in a food processor with the softened butter. Process until smooth. Scrape the Stilton butter into a small bowl.

2 Stir in the 15ml/1 tbsp chives, with the thyme and garlic. Season to taste. Stilton is salty, so you will probably only need to add pepper. Preheat the oven to 180°C/350°F/Gas 4.

3 Place the butter on a piece of foil and shape into an oblong. Wrap this in the foil and seal tightly. Chill the butter by placing it in the refrigerator until it is firm.

4 Brush a sheet of foil, large enough to enclose all the steaks, with olive oil. Support the foil on a baking sheet. Place the steaks on the foil, drizzle the wine over, season and seal the foil tightly. Bake for 20–30 minutes or until cooked through.

5 Unwrap the chilled butter and cut it into four equal portions. Remove the salmon from the oven, carefully open the package and use a fish slice (metal spatula) to transfer each steak to a warmed serving plate. Top each salmon steak with a portion of butter and garnish with the extra chives. Serve immediately with new potatoes, stir-fried red and yellow peppers and mangetouts.

Nutritional information per portion: Energy 604kcal/2508kJ; Protein 47g; Carbohydrate 1g, of which sugars 0g; Fat 45g, of which saturates 15g; Cholesterol 141mg; Calcium 148mg; Fibre 0g; Sodium 355mg.

Baked salmon with herbed mayonnaise

Cooking the salmon in foil produces a moist result, rather like poaching. The traditional covering of thin slices of cucumber with lemon slices gives the dish a wonderful retro look.

SERVES 6–8

2–3kg/4½–6¾lb salmon, cleaned, with
    head and tail left on
3–5 spring onions (scallions), thinly sliced
1 lemon, thinly sliced
600ml/1 pint/2½ cups good-quality
    mayonnaise, mixed with chopped
    mixed herbs such as parsley, dill,
    chives or chervil, chilled
finely sliced cucumber and lemon slices,
    to garnish

1 Preheat the oven to 180°C/350°F/ Gas 4. Lay the salmon on a large piece of foil. Stuff with spring onions and layer the lemon slices in and around the fish. Season, fold the foil around the fish, and bake for 1 hour. Remove the salmon from the oven and leave to stand for 15 minutes, then unwrap the foil and leave to cool completely.

2 When cool, lift the salmon on to a large plate. Cover tightly with plastic wrap and chill for several hours.

3 Use a blunt knife to carefully peel the skin away from the flesh, avoiding tearing the flesh. Transfer to a platter, cover with cucumber slices, surround with lemon slices, and serve with the mayonnaise.

Nutritional information per portion: Energy 783kcal/3242kJ; Protein 38.7g; Carbohydrate 1g, of which sugars 0.9g; Fat 69.3g, of which saturates 21.3g; Cholesterol 173mg; Calcium 102mg; Fibre 0.5g; Sodium 418mg.

Herring fillets with caper butter sauce

This recipe is a modern take on a traditional recipe using Baltic herrings. The flavour of the ubiquitous dill adds that authentic Scandinavian flavour to this otherwise simple dish.

SERVES 4

a little butter, for greasing
50g/2oz/1 cup fine fresh breadcrumbs
600g/1lb 6oz Baltic herring fillets
salt

FOR THE CAPER BUTTER
100g/3 ³⁄₄oz/scant ¹⁄₂ cup butter,
    softened
15ml/1 tbsp vodka
30ml/2 tbsp chopped fresh dill
15ml/1 tbsp capers
1 large pinch cayenne pepper

1 Preheat the oven to 200°C/ 400°F/Gas 6. Grease a shallow, ovenproof dish with butter and sprinkle 15ml/1 tbsp of the breadcrumbs over the base.

2 To make the caper butter, put the softened butter in a bowl and beat until it is light and fluffy, then whisk in the vodka, dill, capers and cayenne pepper.

3 Season the fish with salt then fold each fillet in half, so that the skin sides are on the outside. Lightly press the folded fish together with your fingers. Place in the dish, spread the caper butter over and top with the remaining breadcrumbs.

4 Bake the fish in the oven for 25 minutes or until the top is crisp and golden brown.

Nutritional information per portion: Energy 545kcal/2261kJ; Protein 28.6g; Carbohydrate 10.1g, of which sugars 0.7g; Fat 42.8g, of which saturates 19.3g; Cholesterol 134mg; Calcium 126mg; Fibre 0.7g; Sodium 444mg.

Pies and Gratins

Fish and pastry have a real affinity, and fish pie must be one of the most comforting and homely dishes there is. There are many versions, all of them delicious. A protective covering, whether of pastry, potato or a sauce, means the fish cooks without losing moisture. Ideal for meals where a little fish needs to go further, these bakes and gratins will become firm favourites.

Seafood pie with rösti topping

This oven-baked dish is a mixture of white fish and shellfish with a creamy sauce, finished with a grated potato topping that gives texture and lightness to the dish.

SERVES 4

750g/1lb 10oz potatoes, unpeeled and scrubbed
50g/2oz/¼ cup butter, melted
350g/12oz cod or haddock fillets, skinned
   and cut into bitesize pieces
115g/4oz cooked, peeled prawns (shrimp)
115g/4oz cooked, shelled mussels
8–12 shelled queen scallops
50g/2oz/¼ cup butter
1 onion, finely chopped

50g/2oz/½ cup plain (all-purpose) flour
200ml/7fl oz/scant 1 cup dry white wine
300ml/½ pint/1¼ cups fish or vegetable stock
105ml/7 tbsp double (heavy) cream
30ml/2 tbsp chopped fresh dill, plus extra
   sprigs, to garnish
15ml/1 tbsp chopped fresh parsley
60ml/4 tbsp freshly grated Parmesan cheese
salt and ground black pepper

1 Place the potatoes in a large pan. Cover with cold water and bring to the boil. Cook for 10–15 minutes until just tender.

2 Drain the potatoes and set aside until cool enough to handle. Peel and coarsely grate the cooled potatoes into a bowl. Stir in the melted butter and season well with salt and pepper.

3 Preheat the oven to 220°C/425°F/Gas 7. Divide the pieces of cod or haddock and the prawns, mussels and scallops among four individual 18cm/7in rectangular ovenproof dishes.

4 Melt the butter in a large pan, add the onion and cook for 6–8 minutes or until softened and light golden. Sprinkle in the flour and stir thoroughly until well blended.

5 Remove the pan from the heat and pour in the wine and stock, stirring until smooth. Bring to the boil, then stir in the cream, herbs and season to taste. Pour the sauce over the fish.

6 Sprinkle the potato evenly over the fish and sauce in the dishes and top with Parmesan cheese. Bake for 25 minutes until the topping is crisp and the fish is cooked. Serve hot, garnished with dill.

Nutritional information per portion: Energy 770kcal/3215kJ; Protein 47.3g; Carbohydrate 44.5g, of which sugars 4.5g; Fat 42.4g, of which saturates 25.5g; Cholesterol 236mg; Calcium 298mg; Fibre 2.7g; Sodium 626mg.

Salt cod with potato mash gratin

This recipe is reminiscent of the well-known French salt cod purée, brandade. Many similar dishes are produced in other Mediterranean countries, using salt or dried cod, also known as stockfish.

SERVES 8

1kg/2¼lb potatoes, unpeeled
800g/1¾lb salt cod, soaked
105ml/7 tbsp olive oil
200ml/7fl oz/scant 1 cup single (light)
    cream
2 garlic cloves, chopped
a small bunch of parsley, chopped
pinch of freshly grated nutmeg
salt

COOK'S TIP

Salt cod can often be bought from Italian and Spanish groceries, as well as from Greek food stores.

1 Cook the potatoes in a large pan of lightly salted boiling water for 20–30 minutes, until tender. Drain well, then peel and mash with a fork. Meanwhile, preheat the oven to 200°C/400°F/Gas 6.

2 Bring another large pan of water to the boil. Add the fish and bring back to the boil, then immediately remove the pan from the heat. Leave to stand for 5 minutes.

3 Remove the fish from the pan with a slotted spatula and leave to cool slightly. Remove and discard the skin and bones. Mix the fish with the potatoes, then blend in the olive oil and cream and the garlic. Stir in the parsley and nutmeg and season with salt, if necessary.

4 Spoon the mixture into an ovenproof dish and bake for about 20 minutes. Serve hot.

Nutritional information per portion: Energy 366kcal/1535kJ; Protein 35.9g; Carbohydrate 21.4g, of which sugars 2.4g; Fat 15.8g, of which saturates 4.7g; Cholesterol 73mg; Calcium 65mg; Fibre 1.7g; Sodium 423mg.

Baked salt cod with potatoes, tomatoes and olives

Salt cod has been a winter staple in Greece for generations. It is particularly popular in the spring, and this particular dish is often on the menu at city restaurants on Fridays during Lent.

SERVES 4

675g/1½ lb salt cod
800g/1¾lb potatoes, peeled and cut into
    small wedges
1 large onion, finely chopped
2–3 garlic cloves, chopped
leaves from a fresh rosemary sprig
30ml/2 tbsp chopped fresh flat leaf
    parsley
120ml/4fl oz/½ cup extra virgin olive oil
400g/14oz can chopped tomatoes
15ml/1 tbsp tomato purée (paste)
300ml/½ pint/1¼ cups hot water
5ml/1 tsp dried oregano
12 black olives
ground black pepper

1 Soak the cod in cold water overnight, changing the water as often as possible in the course of the evening and the following day. The cod does not have to be skinned for this dish, but you should remove any obvious fins or bones.

2 Preheat the oven to 180°C/ 350°F/Gas 4. Mix the potatoes, onion, garlic, rosemary and parsley in a large roasting pan. Grind over plenty of pepper. Add the olive oil and toss to coat. Drain the cod and cut it into serving pieces.

3 Arrange the pieces of cod between the vegetables, and spread with the tomatoes. Stir the tomato purée into the hot water until dissolved, then pour the mixture over the contents of the tin. Sprinkle the oregano on top. Bake for 1 hour, basting the fish and potatoes occasionally with the pan juices.

4 Remove the roasting pan from the oven, sprinkle the olives on top, then cook it for 30 minutes more, adding more hot water if needed. Garnish with fresh herbs. Serve hot or cold.

Nutritional information per portion: Energy 692kcal/2886kJ; Protein 55g; Carbohydrate 43g, of which sugars 8g; Fat 33g, of which saturates 4g; Cholesterol 0mg; Calcium 431mg; Fibre 5g; Sodium 267mg.

Seafood pie

A well-made fish pie is absolutely delicious, and is particularly good made with a mixture of fresh and smoked fish. Cooked shellfish, such as mussels, can be included too.

SERVES 4–5

450g/1lb haddock or cod fillet and
225g/8oz smoked haddock or cod, cut
into bitesize pieces
150ml/¼ pint/⅔ cup milk
150ml/¼ pint/⅔ cup water
1 slice of lemon
1 small bay leaf
a few fresh parsley stalks

FOR THE SAUCE

25g/1oz/2 tbsp butter
25g/1oz/¼ cup plain (all-purpose) flour
5ml/1 tbsp lemon juice, or to taste
45ml/3 tbsp chopped fresh parsley
ground black pepper

FOR THE TOPPING

450g/1lb potatoes, boiled and mashed
with 25g/1oz/2 tbsp butter

1 Preheat the oven to 190°C/375°F/ Gas 5. Place the fish into a pan with the milk, water, lemon, bay leaf and parsley stalks. Bring slowly to the boil, then simmer for 5–8 minutes until partly cooked. Strain and reserve 300ml/½ pint/1¼ cups of the cooking liquor. Leave the fish to cool, then flake the flesh and discard the skin and bones. Set aside.

2 To make the sauce, melt the butter in a heavy pan, add the flour and cook for 1–2 minutes over low heat, stirring. Gradually add the reserved cooking liquor, stirring well to make a smooth sauce.

3 Simmer the sauce gently for 1–2 minutes, then remove from the heat and stir in the flaked fish, chopped parsley and lemon juice. Season to taste. Turn into a buttered 1.75 litre/ 3 pint/7½ cup pie dish or shallow casserole, cover with the potato topping.

4 Cook in the oven for about 20 minutes, or until thoroughly heated through. The top should be golden brown and crunchy. Divide the pie among 4–5 warmed plates and serve with a lightly cooked green vegetable, such as fresh broccoli spears.

Nutritional information per portion: Energy 336Kcal/1413kJ; Protein 35.1g; Carbohydrate 24.3g, of which sugars 0.9g; Fat 11.6g, of which saturates 6.7g; Cholesterol 87mg; Calcium 45mg; Fibre 1.7g; Sodium 587mg.

Fish pie with saffron mash

This is the ultimate fish pie. Breaking through the golden potato crust reveals prawns and chunks of cod swathed in a creamy parsley sauce.

SERVES 6

750ml/1¼ pints/3 cups milk
1 onion, chopped
1 bay leaf
2–3 peppercorns
450g/1lb each of fresh cod fillet and
   smoked haddock fillet
350g/12oz cooked tiger prawns (jumbo
   shrimp), shelled
75g/3oz/6 tbsp butter
75g/3oz/¾ cup plain (all-purpose) flour
60ml/4 tbsp chopped fresh parsley
1.3kg/3lb floury potatoes, peeled
a large pinch of saffron threads, soaked in
   45ml/3 tbsp hot water
75g/3oz/6 tbsp butter
250ml/8fl oz/1 cup milk
45ml/3 tbsp chopped fresh dill
salt and ground black pepper

1 Put the milk, onion, bay leaf and peppercorns into a pan. Bring to the boil and simmer for 10 minutes. Lay the fish fillets, skin side up, in a separate pan. Add the milk and simmer for 5–7 minutes. Lift the fish out of the pan and strain the milk.

2 When the fish is cool, pull off the skin and flake the flesh into large pieces, removing any bones as you go. Transfer to a large bowl and add the shelled prawns.

3 Melt the butter in a pan. Stir in the flour, cook for 1 minute, then gradually stir in the reserved milk.

4 Whisk well and simmer gently for 15 minutes until thick and a little reduced, then taste and season with salt and pepper. Stir in the parsley. Pour the sauce over the fish, transfer to a pie dish and leave to cool.

5 Preheat the oven to 180°C/350°F/Gas 4. Boil the potatoes in salted water until tender, drain and mash until smooth. Beat in the saffron and its soaking water, then the butter, milk and dill.

6 When the fish mixture has cooled and set, pile the mash on top. Bake for 30–40 minutes until golden.

Nutritional information per portion: Energy 458kcal/1921kJ; Protein 29.4g; Carbohydrate 32.8g, of which sugars 5.8g; Fat 25g, of which saturates 3.7g; Cholesterol 74mg; Calcium 216mg; Fibre 1g; Sodium 867mg.

Fish pie

This traditional fish pie, using a combination of white fish and smoked haddock, is given a Welsh flavour with the addition of laverbread, a spinach-like puree made from laver – a seaweed found on the coast of Wales. You can buy it online, or replace it with dried nori seaweed.

SERVES 4

225g/8oz skinless white fish, such as hake, haddock or cod
225g/8oz skinless smoked haddock or cod
425ml/³/₄ pint/scant 2 cups milk
25g/1oz/2 tbsp butter
25g/1oz/¹/₂ cup plain (all-purpose) flour
good pinch of freshly grated nutmeg

1 leek, thinly sliced
200g/7oz shelled cooked cockles (small clam)
30ml/2 tbsp laverbread or dried nori seaweed
30ml/2 tbsp finely chopped fresh parsley
1 sheet ready-rolled puff pastry
salt and ground black pepper
beaten egg, or milk, for brushing

1 Preheat the oven to 200°C/400°F/Gas 6. Put the white and smoked fish in a pan with the milk. Heat until the milk barely comes to the boil, then cover and poach gently for about 8 minutes or until the fish is just cooked. Lift the fish out, reserving the liquid. Break into flakes, discarding any bones.

2 Melt the butter, stir in the flour and cook for 1–2 minutes. Remove from the heat and gradually stir in the reserved cooking liquid, stirring continuously, and heat until the sauce thickens.

3 Stir the fish flakes and their juices in to the sauce. Add nutmeg and season to taste. Add the leek, cockles, laverbread, if using, and parsley to the sauce, and spoon into a 1.2 litre/2 pint/5 cup ovenproof dish.

4 Brush the edges of the dish with water. Unroll the pastry and lay it over the top of the dish, trimming it to fit. Use the pastry off-cuts to make decorative fish or leaves for the top, brushing each one with a little water to help them stick. Brush over the pastry top with beaten egg or milk.

5 Place the pie into the hot oven and cook for about 30 minutes, or until the pastry is puffed and golden brown. Serve hot.

Nutritional information per portion: Energy 573kcal/2401kJ; Protein 36.8g; Carbohydrate 41g, of which sugars 7.3g; Fat 31.2g, of which saturates 4.7g; Cholesterol 92mg; Calcium 270mg; Fibre 1.2g; Sodium 1084mg.

Trout and asparagus pie

Crisp filo pastry filled with layers of trout, ricotta cheese, asparagus and mushrooms makes a dramatic and elegant dish that is extremely easy to make.

SERVES 6–8

75g/3oz/6 tbsp butter

1 small onion, chopped

115g/4oz/1½ cups button (white) mushrooms, sliced

30ml/2 tbsp chopped fresh flat leaf parsley

250g/9oz/generous 1 cup ricotta cheese

115g/4oz/½ cup mascarpone

450g/1lb trout fillet, skinned and pin bones removed

8 filo pastry sheets, each measuring 45 x 25cm/18 x 10in

115g/4oz asparagus, blanched for 3 minutes, drained and refreshed

salt and ground black pepper

butter, for greasing

1 Preheat the oven to 200°C/400°F/Gas 6. Grease a 23cm/9in springform cake tin (pan).

2 Heat 25g/1oz/2 tbsp of the butter in a frying pan and add the onion. Cook for 3–5 minutes or until soft. Add the mushrooms and cook for 2 minutes more. Stir in the parsley and season with salt and pepper.

3 In a bowl, combine the ricotta cheese and mascarpone. Stir in the onion mixture. Melt the remaining butter in a pan. Line the cake tin with filo sheets, brushing each layer with melted butter and leaving the edges to hang over the sides.

4 While you are working with one filo pastry sheet, keep the rest covered with a damp, clean dish towel. Place half the ricotta mixture in the base of the filo-lined tin. Arrange the trout fillets in a layer over the ricotta. Season well.

5 Top with the blanched asparagus and the remaining ricotta mixture. Bring the overhanging edges of the pastry over the top, and brush the layers with the remaining butter.

6 Bake the pie for 25 minutes. Cover with foil and cook for a further 15 minutes. Remove from the tin and place on a plate. Serve in slices.

Nutritional information per portion: Energy 310kcal/1293kJ; Protein 17g; Carbohydrate 13g, of which sugars 3g; Fat 21g, of which saturates 12g; Cholesterol 87mg; Calcium 109mg; Fibre 1g; Sodium 236mg.

Filo-wrapped fish

This delicious dish comes from Jerusalem, where many types of fish are typically wrapped in filo pastry and served with a zesty tomato sauce.

SERVES 4

450g/1lb salmon or cod steaks

1 lemon

30ml/2 tbsp olive oil, plus extra, for brushing

1 onion, chopped

2 celery sticks, chopped

1 green (bell) pepper, diced

5 garlic cloves, chopped

400g/14oz fresh or canned tomatoes, chopped

120ml/4fl oz/½ cup passata (bottled strained tomatoes)

30ml/2 tbsp chopped fresh flat leaf parsley

2–3 pinches of ground allspice or ground cloves

cayenne pepper, to taste

a pinch of sugar

130g/4½ oz filo pastry (8 large sheets)

salt and ground black pepper

1 Sprinkle the salmon or cod steaks with salt and black pepper and a squeeze of lemon juice. Set aside and prepare the sauce.

2 Heat the olive oil in a pan, add the chopped onion, celery and pepper and fry for about 5 minutes, until the vegetables are softened. Stir in the garlic, then add the tomatoes and passata and cook until reduced.

3 Stir the parsley into the sauce, then season with allspice or cloves, cayenne pepper, sugar and salt and pepper. Preheat the oven to 200°C/400°F/Gas 6.

4 Take a sheet of filo pastry, brush with a little olive oil and cover with a second sheet. Place a piece of fish on top of the pastry, toward the bottom edge, then top with 1–2 spoonfuls of the sauce.

5 Roll the fish in the pastry. Place the parcel on a baking sheet and repeat with the remaining fish and pastry. You should have about half the sauce remaining.

6 Bake in the oven for 10–15 minutes, or until golden. Reheat the remaining sauce if necessary. Serve with the remaining sauce.

Nutritional information per portion: Energy 496kcal/2063kJ; Protein 20.6g; Carbohydrate 26.7g, of which sugars 1.3g; Fat 34.8g, of which saturates 8.1g; Cholesterol 249mg; Calcium 111mg; Fibre 1.5g; Sodium 217mg.

Smoked haddock flan

The classic combination of potatoes and smoked fish is reworked here in pastry to make a lovely creamy-textured filling that is complemented by the crisp case.

SERVES 4

FOR THE PASTRY

225g/8oz/2 cups plain (all-purpose) flour
pinch of salt
115g/4oz/1½ cup cold butter, diced
cold water, to mix

FOR THE FILLING

200g/7oz undyed smoked haddock fillets
600ml/1 pint/2½ cups full-fat (whole) milk
3–4 black peppercorns
sprig of fresh thyme
150ml/¼ pint/²⁄₃ cup double (heavy) cream
2 eggs
200g/7oz potatoes, diced
ground black pepper

1 Preheat the oven to 200°C/400°F/Gas 6. Put the flour, salt and butter into a processor, and process until it resembles fine breadcrumbs.

2 Pour in a little cold water (about 40ml/8 tsp) and continue to process until the mixture forms a ball. If this takes longer than 30 seconds, add a dash or two more water.

3 Wrap the pastry ball in clear film (plastic wrap) and leave to rest in a cool place for about 30 minutes. Roll out the dough and use to line a 20cm/8in flan tin (quiche pan).

4 Prick the base of the pastry all over with a fork, then bake blind in the preheated oven for 20 minutes.

5 Put the haddock in a pan with the milk, peppercorns and thyme. Poach for 10 minutes. Remove the fish from the pan and flake into chunks.

6 Whisk the cream and eggs together, then whisk in the cooled poaching milk. Layer the flan case with the fish and potato, season with pepper. Pour the cream mixture in and bake for 40 minutes. Serve warm.

Nutritional information per portion: Energy 734kcal/3064kJ; Protein 23.8g; Carbohydrate 58.4g, of which sugars 8.2g; Fat 46.8g, of which saturates 27.9g; Cholesterol 225mg; Calcium 280mg; Fibre 2.3g; Sodium 636mg.

Salmon and prawn tart

This tart is unusual because it is made with raw salmon, which means that the fish stays moist. Cooking it this way gives a lovely succulent result. Serve the tart warm with a mixed salad.

SERVES 6

350g/12oz shortcrust pastry, thawed if frozen
225g/8oz salmon fillet, skinned
225g/8oz/2 cups cooked peeled prawns (shrimp)
2 eggs, plus 2 egg yolks
150ml/¼ pint/⅔ cup whipping cream
200ml/7fl oz/scant 1 cup milk
15ml/1 tbsp chopped fresh dill
salt, ground black pepper and paprika
tomato salad, to serve

1 Roll out the pastry and use it to line a 20cm/8in quiche dish or tin (pan). Prick the base all over and mark the edges with the tines of the fork. It need not be too neat. Chill for about 30 minutes.

2 Meanwhile, preheat the oven to 180°C/350°F/Gas 4. Bake the pastry case (pie shell) for 30 minutes, until golden brown. Reduce the oven temperature to 160°C/325°F/Gas 3.

3 Cut the salmon into 2cm/¾in cubes. Arrange the salmon and prawns evenly in the pastry case. Dust with paprika.

4 In a bowl, beat together the eggs and yolks, cream, milk and dill, and season. Pour over the salmon and prawns. Bake for 30 minutes, until the filling is just set. Serve hot or at room temperature, with a fresh tomato salad.

Nutritional information per portion: Energy 517kcal/2151kJ; Protein 22g; Carbohydrate 29g, of which sugars 3g; Fat 35g, of which saturates 14g; Cholesterol 242mg; Calcium 159mg; Fibre 1g; Sodium 372mg.

Egg and salmon puff parcels

These elegant parcels conceal a mouthwatering mixture of flavours, and make a delicious appetizer or lunch dish. Serve with curry-flavoured mayonnaise or hollandaise sauce.

SERVES 6

75g/3oz/scant ½ cup long grain rice, cooked according to the instructions on the packet, but in fish stock instead of water
350g/12oz tail pieces of salmon
juice of ½ lemon
15ml/1 tbsp chopped fresh dill
15ml/1 tbsp chopped fresh parsley
10ml/2 tsp mild curry powder
6 small eggs, soft-boiled and cooled and peeled
425g/15oz ready-made puff pastry
1 egg, beaten
salt and ground black pepper

1 Preheat the oven to 220°C/425°F/Gas 7. Place the salmon in a large pan and cover with cold water. Heat until the water is not quite simmering for 8–10 minutes until it flakes easily when tested.

2 Lift the salmon out of the pan and remove the bones and skin. Flake the fish into the rice, add the lemon juice, herbs, curry powder and seasoning, and mix well.

3 Roll out the pastry and cut into six 15cm/6in squares. Brush the edges with the beaten egg.

4 Place a spoonful of the rice mixture in the middle of each square, push an egg into the centre and top with a little more of the rice mixture. Pull over the pastry corners to the middle to form a neat parcel. Press the joins firmly together with your fingers to seal.

5 Brush the parcels with beaten egg, place on a baking sheet and bake for 20 minutes, then reduce the oven temperature to 190°C/375°F/Gas 5. Cook for 10 minutes more or until golden and crisp underneath. Cool the pastries slightly before serving.

Nutritional information per portion: Energy 494kcal/2063kJ; Protein 23.4g; Carbohydrate 36.9g, of which sugars 1.1g; Fat 29.7g, of which saturates 2.7g; Cholesterol 219mg; Calcium 112mg; Fibre 0.8g; Sodium 326mg.

Thai-style seafood pasties

Food from Thailand is popular along the west coast of America, where rice is one of the most important crops. These little pastries are utterly delicious.

MAKES 18

275g/10oz skinned white fish fillets, such as cod or haddock, cubed
plain (all-purpose) flour, seasoned
8–10 raw prawns (shrimp), peeled and deveined
15ml/1 tbsp sunflower oil
50g/2oz/3 tbsp butter
6 spring onions (scallions), finely sliced
1 garlic clove, crushed
225g/8oz/2 cups cooked jasmine rice
4cm/1½in piece fresh root ginger, grated
10ml/2 tsp chopped fresh coriander (cilantro)
5ml/1 tsp finely grated lime rind
500g/1¼lb puff pastry, thawed if frozen
1 egg, beaten with 30ml/2 tbsp water
coriander (cilantro) leaves and lime slices, to garnish

1 Preheat the oven to 190°C/375°F/Gas 5. Dust the fish cubes with the flour. Heat half of the oil and half the butter in a frying pan.

2 Add the spring onions to the frying pan and fry for 2 minutes, stirring. Add the garlic and fry for about 2 minutes more, until soft. Transfer to a large bowl.

3 Heat the remaining oil and butter in the pan. Fry the fish pieces briefly and then add them to the bowl. Cook the prawns in the pan until turning pink, then add to the bowl.

4 Add the rice, ginger, coriander and lime rind to the bowl. Mix well with your hands.

5 Dust the work surface with flour. Roll out the pastry and cut into 10cm/4in rounds. Place spoonfuls of filling on the pastry rounds, and dot with butter. Dampen the edges of the pastry with the egg wash, fold one side of the pastry over the filling and press together firmly.

6 Place on a greased baking sheet. Brush with egg wash and bake for 12–15 minutes. Serve warm.

Nutritional information per portion: Energy 171kcal/715kJ; Protein 8.6g; Carbohydrate 18.7g, of which sugars 0.9g; Fat 7g, of which saturates 2.3g; Cholesterol 48mg; Calcium 34mg; Fibre 0.4g; Sodium 99mg.

Stuffed lemon sole with gratin sauce

These mushroom-stuffed fillets of white fish are a modern take on a traditional recipe. A light Parmesan and tarragon sauce makes a succulent topping for the stuffed fish.

SERVES 4

4 large lemon sole fillets (or any other white fish fillet), about 200g/7oz each, skinned and bones removed
10g/¼oz/½ tbsp butter
300g/11oz wild mushrooms, finely chopped
5ml/1 tsp finely chopped fresh tarragon
60ml/4 tbsp white wine
60ml/4 tbsp double (heavy) cream
salt and ground black pepper

FOR THE SAUCE

7.5ml/1½ tsp butter
1 shallot, finely chopped
15ml/1 tbsp cornflour (cornstarch)
200ml/7fl oz/scant 1 cup fish stock
115g/4oz/1¼ cups freshly grated Parmesan cheese
15ml/1 tbsp finely chopped fresh tarragon

1 Lay the fish fillets on a board or work surface, skin side down. Season with salt and pepper and set aside.

2 Melt the butter in a pan and add the mushrooms. Stir for 4–5 minutes, then add the tarragon. Add the wine and cream, and cook 5–6 more minutes, or until the liquid has evaporated. Remove from the heat and allow to cool.

3 Preheat the oven to 180°C/350°F/Gas 4. Divide the mushroom mixture among the fish fillets, spreading it along the fillets. Roll up the fillets, making sure that the mushroom filling remains tucked inside. Secure the rolls with cocktail sticks (toothpicks) and arrange in an ovenproof dish just large enough to hold the fish.

4 To make the sauce, melt the butter and add the shallot. Sauté for 1–2 minutes. Stir in the cornflour, then gradually add the stock, and combine well to make a smooth sauce.

5 Cook over a low heat for 5 minutes, then add the Parmesan and tarragon. Pour the sauce over the fillets and bake for 20–25 minutes, or until golden brown. Remove from the oven and serve.

Nutritional information per portion: Energy 420kcal/1757kJ; Protein 46g; Carbohydrate 5.1g, of which sugars 1.3g; Fat 23.9g, of which saturates 13.2g; Cholesterol 178mg; Calcium 393mg; Fibre 0.2g; Sodium 545mg.

Salmon, potato and mushroom bake

This layered bake is rich, filling and delicious. The hint of caraway goes surprisingly well with the salmon and mushrooms. Make this in a large casserole, and cook for 35–45 minutes, if you wish.

SERVES 4–6

135ml/4½ fl oz/scant ²⁄₃ cup vegetable oil

4 waxy potatoes, peeled and thinly sliced

10g/¼oz/½ tbsp butter, plus extra for greasing

300g/11oz/generous 4 cups mushrooms, thinly sliced

1 large onion, finely sliced in rings

1.5ml/½ tsp caraway seeds

500g/1¼lb thin salmon fillets, bones and skin removed

2 large eggs, beaten

300ml/½ pint/1¼ cups single (light) cream

200g/7oz/3½ cups fresh rye breadcrumbs

salt and ground black pepper

1 Preheat the oven to 180°C/350°F/ Gas 4. Heat 75–90ml/5–6 tbsp oil in a large non-stick frying pan over a medium heat. Add the potatoes a few at a time, and cook for 5–8 minutes, or until they are almost tender and lightly browned. Remove with a slotted spoon and set aside.

2 Add the butter to the pan and add the mushrooms. Sauté for about 4 minutes, or until soft. Season to taste and remove the mushrooms from the pan.

3 Add the remaining oil to the pan and cook the onion rings for 4–5 minutes, until lightly browned.

4 Line buttered individual serving dishes with most of the pre-cooked potatoes in a solid layer, overlapping the slices slightly.

5 Spoon over the mushrooms, and then top with the onion rings. Grind the caraway seeds using a mortar and pestle, and sprinkle over the top. Top with the salmon fillets and finish with a layer of potatoes.

6 Combine the eggs and cream in a bowl and season with salt and pepper. Pour over the surface. Sprinkle the top with breadcrumbs. Bake for 20–25 minutes, or until golden brown. Serve hot.

Nutritional information per portion: Energy 689kcal/2877kJ; Protein 27.2g; Carbohydrate 57.6g, of which sugars 7.1g; Fat 40.4g, of which saturates 11.2g; Cholesterol 149mg; Calcium 144mg; Fibre 3.4g; Sodium 422mg.

Creamy anchovy and potato bake

This classic Scandinavian dish of potatoes, onions and anchovies cooked with cream makes a hearty winter lunch or simple supper, served with a refreshing salad.

SERVES 4

1kg/2¼ lb maincrop potatoes
2 onions
25g/1oz/2 tbsp butter
2 x 50g/2oz cans anchovy fillets
150ml/¼ pint/⅔ cup single (light) cream
150ml/¼ pint/⅔ cup double (heavy) cream
15ml/1 tbsp chopped fresh parsley
ground black pepper
fresh crusty bread, to serve

COOK'S TIP

This recipe can also be served as an appetizer for six, or as a side dish to accompany a main meal.

1 Peel the potatoes and cut into slices slightly thicker than 1cm/½in. Cut the slices into strips slightly more than 1cm/½in wide. Peel the onions and cut into very thin rings.

2 Use half of the butter to grease a ceramic cooking pot, and layer half the potatoes and onions in the base.

3 Drain the anchovies, reserving 15ml/1 tbsp of the oil. Cut the anchovies into thin strips and lay these over the potatoes and onions, then layer the remaining potatoes and onions on top.

4 Combine the single cream and anchovy oil in a small jug (pitcher) and season with a little ground black pepper. Pour the mixture evenly over the potatoes and dot with butter.

5 Cover and cook on high for 3½ hours, or until the potatoes and onions are tender.

6 Finish by browning the top under a hot grill (broiler), if you like, then drizzle over the double cream and sprinkle with parsley and pepper. Serve with fresh crusty bread.

Nutritional information per portion: Energy 378Kcal/1580kJ; Protein 11.3g; Carbohydrate 37.9g, of which sugars 6.4g; Fat 21.2g, of which saturates 11.4g; Cholesterol 54mg; Calcium 1460mg; Fibre 11.5g; Sodium 133mg.

Gratin of cod with mustard

This is an incredibly quick and easy dish to make. You can now buy good-quality farmed cod, but if you need an alternative, then select a thick, flaky-textured, moist white-fleshed fish.

SERVES 4

4 cod steaks, approximately 175g/6oz
    each
200g/7oz/1³/4 cups grated Cheddar
    cheese, such as Isle of Mull
15ml/1 tbsp wholegrain mustard
75ml/5 tbsp double (heavy) cream
salt and ground black pepper

VARIATION
*If you don't have wholegrain mustard,
use any ready-made mustard.*

1 Preheat the oven to 200°C/ 400°F/Gas 6. Check the fish for bones and remove any pin bones with tweezers. Butter an ovenproof dish then place the fish fillets skin side down in the dish and season.

2 In a small bowl, mix the grated cheese and mustard together with enough cream to form a paste.

3 Season the cheese mixture lightly, then spread thickly and evenly over each fish fillet, using it all up.

4 Bake in the preheated oven for about 15–20 minutes, until the top of the gratin is browned and bubbling and the fish underneath is flaky and tender. Serve immediately on warmed plates.

Nutritional information per portion: Energy 445kcal/1852kJ; Protein 46g; Carbohydrate 9.1g, of which sugars 2.2g; Fat 14g, of which saturates 8.2g; Cholesterol 84mg; Calcium 170mg; Fibre 1.7g; Sodium 213mg.

Smoked mussel and potato bake

This slow-baked dish uses smoked mussels, which have a creamy texture and rich flavour, delicious with sour cream and chives. You can substitute smoked oysters for the mussels.

SERVES 4

2 large maincrop potatoes, cut in half
butter, for greasing
2 shallots, finely diced
2 x 85g/3¼oz cans smoked mussels
1 bunch chives, chopped
300ml/½ pint/1¼ cups sour cream
175g/6oz/1½ cups mature Cheddar
   cheese, grated
salt and ground black pepper
mixed vegetables, to serve

1 Preheat the oven to 180°C/ 350°F/Gas 4. Cook the potatoes in a large pan of lightly salted boiling water for 15 minutes until they are just tender. Drain and leave to cool slightly. When cool enough to handle, cut the potatoes into even 3mm/⅛in slices.

2 Grease the base and sides of a 1.2 litre/2 pint/5 cup casserole dish. Lay a few potato slices over the base of the dish. Sprinkle a few shallots over and season well.

3 Drain the oil from the mussels into a bowl. Slice the mussels and return to the reserved oil. Stir in the chives and sour cream with half of the cheese. Spoon a little of the sauce over the layer of potatoes.

4 Continue to layer the potatoes, shallots and the sauce in the dish. Finish with a layer of potatoes and sprinkle over the rest of the cheese. Bake for 30–45 minutes. Remove from the oven and serve hot with a selection of vegetables.

Nutritional information per portion: Energy 348kcal/1457kJ; Protein 16.7g; Carbohydrate 25.8g, of which sugars 3.4g; Fat 20.6g, of which saturates 3g; Cholesterol 30mg; Calcium 178mg; Fibre 1.8g; Sodium 288mg.

Prawns with tomatoes and feta

This luxurious and unusual dish is traditionally cooked in a round earthenware dish without a lid. Serve it as a first course for six, with plenty of crusty bread, or with rice as a main course for four.

SERVES 4

75ml/5 tbsp extra virgin olive oil
1 onion, chopped
½ red (bell) pepper, seeded and cubed
675g/1½ lb ripe tomatoes, peeled and roughly chopped
generous pinch of sugar
2.5ml/½ tsp dried oregano
450g/1lb peeled (but with the tail shells intact) raw tiger or king prawns (jumbo shrimp), thawed if frozen
30ml/2 tbsp finely chopped fresh flat leaf parsley
75g/3oz feta cheese, cubed
salt and ground black pepper

1 Heat the oil in a frying pan, add the onion and sauté gently for a few minutes until translucent. Add the cubed red pepper and cook, stirring occasionally, for 2–3 minutes more.

2 Stir in the chopped tomatoes, sugar and oregano, then season with salt and pepper to taste.

3 Cook gently over a low heat for about 15 minutes, stirring occasionally, until the sauce reduces slightly and thickens.

4 Preheat the oven to 180°C/ 350°F/Gas 4. Stir the prawns and parsley into the tomato sauce, transfer to a baking dish and spread evenly. Sprinkle the cheese cubes on top, then bake for 30 minutes. Serve hot, with a fresh green salad.

COOK'S TIP

Feta is a Greek cheese that is traditionally made from ewes' milk, but now is often made from cow's milk. It is preserved in brine and has a slightly salty taste and crumbly texture.

Nutritional information per portion: Energy 328kcal/1362kJ; Protein 19g; Carbohydrate 10g, of which sugars 9g; Fat 24g, of which saturates 6g; Cholesterol 172mg; Calcium 159mg; Fibre 3g; Sodium 442mg.

Octopus and pasta bake

This slow-cooked combination of octopus, not everyone's first choice for seafood, and pasta in a spicy tomato sauce is quite an everyday dish in Greece.

SERVES 4

2 octopuses, total weight about
   675–800g/1½–1¾lb, cleaned
150ml/¼ pint/²⁄₃ cup extra virgin
   olive oil
2 large onions, sliced
3 garlic cloves, chopped
1 fresh red or green chilli, seeded and
   thinly sliced
1–2 bay leaves
5ml/1 tsp dried oregano
1 piece of cinnamon stick
2–3 grains allspice (optional)
1 glass red wine
30ml/2 tbsp tomato purée (paste)
   diluted in 300ml/½ pint/1¼ cups
   warm water
300ml/½ pint/1¼ cups boiling water
225g/8oz/2 cups penne or small dried
   macaroni-type pasta
ground black pepper

1 Rinse the octopuses, cut into large cubes and place in a heavy pan over a low heat. Cook gently; they will produce some liquid, and they will eventually become bright scarlet. Keep turning the pieces of octopus with a wooden spatula until all the liquid has evaporated.

2 Add the olive oil to the pan and sauté the octopus pieces for 4–5 minutes. Add the onions to the pan and cook for a further 4 minutes, stirring, until they turn golden. Stir in the garlic, chilli, bay leaf, oregano, cinnamon stick and allspice, if using.

3 Pour the wine in to the pan, and let it bubble for a couple of minutes. Pour in the diluted tomato purée, add pepper, cover and cook gently for 1½ hours or until the octopus is perfectly soft. Stir occasionally and add a little hot water if needed.

4 Preheat the oven to 160°C/ 325°F/Gas 3. Bring the octopus mixture to the boil, add the boiling water and stir in the dried pasta. Tip the mixture into a roasting pan. Bake for 30–35 minutes, stirring occasionally. Add a little hot water if it starts to look dry. Serve hot.

Nutritional information per portion: Energy 874kcal/3662kJ; Protein 71g; Carbohydrate 53g, of which sugars 10g; Fat 43g, of which saturates 6g; Cholesterol 168mg; Calcium 162mg; Fibre 5g; Sodium 27mg.

Baked crab with garlic and ginger

This is a French-inspired dish with an Asian twist. Use freshly cooked crab meat from your fishmonger or supermarket. Buy it in the shell, if possible, or bake this in individual gratin dishes.

SERVES 4

25g/1oz dried mung bean thread (cellophane) noodles
6 dried cloud ear (wood ear) mushrooms
450g/1lb fresh crab meat
15ml/1 tbsp vegetable oil
10ml/2 tsp Thai fish sauce
2 shallots, finely chopped
2 garlic cloves, finely chopped
2.5cm/1in fresh ginger, peeled and grated
1 small bunch coriander (cilantro), stalks removed, leaves chopped
1 egg, beaten
25g/1oz/2 tbsp butter
salt and ground black pepper
fresh dill fronds, to garnish
Thai fish sauce or soy sauce, to serve

1 Preheat the oven to 180°C/ 350°F/Gas 4. Soak the thread noodles and cloud ear mushrooms separately in bowls of lukewarm water for 15 minutes, then squeeze them dry and chop finely.

2 In a bowl, mix together the chopped noodles and mushrooms with the crab meat. Add the oil, Thai fish sauce, shallots, garlic, ginger and coriander. Season, then stir in the beaten egg.

3 Spoon the mixture into four small crab shells or use individual ovenproof dishes, packing it in tightly, and dot the top of each one with a little butter.

4 Place the shells on a baking tray and cook for about 20 minutes, or until the tops are nicely browned.

5 Garnish with dill and serve with a few drops of fish sauce, or a drizzle of soy sauce, over the top.

Nutritional information per portion: Energy 289Kcal/1206kJ; Protein 26g; Carbohydrate 8g, of which sugars 2g; Fat 17g, of which saturates 5g; Cholesterol 145mg; Calcium 39mg; Fibre 24g; Sodium 800mg.

Crab bake

This Irish recipe is popular all around the coast, where crabs are popular on bar menus, especially as fresh crab open sandwiches. Serve hot with fresh crusty bread, and a side salad.

SERVES 4 AS A FIRST COURSE

225g/8oz cooked white crab meat
juice of ½ lemon
15ml/1 tbsp chopped fresh parsley
20ml/4 tsp dry gin
5ml/1 tsp smooth Dijon mustard
5ml/1 tsp wholegrain Dijon mustard
60ml/4 tbsp grated Parmesan cheese
ground black pepper

FOR THE BÉCHAMEL SAUCE
1 small onion
3 cloves
300ml/½ pint/1¼ cups milk
½ bay leaf
25g/1oz/2 tbsp butter
25g/1oz/¼ cup plain (all-purpose) flour

1 First make an infusion for the béchamel sauce: stud the onion with the cloves, and then put it into a small pan with the milk and bay leaf. Bring slowly to the boil, then allow to infuse (steep) for 15 minutes, and strain.

2 Preheat the oven to 180°C/350°F/Gas 4 and butter four gratin dishes. Toss the crab meat in the lemon juice. Divide it among the dishes and add a pinch of herbs to each. Sprinkle each dish with 5ml/ 1 tsp gin and pepper.

3 Melt the butter for the sauce in a pan, stir in the flour and cook over a low heat for 1–2 minutes. Gradually add the infused milk, stirring, to make a smooth sauce. Simmer over a low heat for 1–2 minutes.

4 Blend the béchamel sauce with the two mustards and use to cover the crab.

5 Sprinkle the cheese on top of the crab, and bake for 20–25 minutes, or until the surface is hot and bubbling. Serve immediately.

Nutritional information per portion: Energy 224Kcal/936kJ; Protein 17.4g; Carbohydrate 9.6g, of which sugars 4.5g; Fat 11.9g, of which saturates 7.4g; Cholesterol 73mg; Calcium 282mg; Fibre 0.4g; Sodium 489mg.

Scottish clam stovies

Clams are now farmed, and are especially successful when grown in Scottish lochs. Limpets or cockles can also be used if you can buy them fresh or collect them yourself along the seashore.

SERVES 4

2.5 litres/4 pints/10 cups clams, washed and soaked overnight in a bucket of fresh cold water, to clean
potatoes (see step 2)
oil, for greasing
chopped fresh flat leaf parsley, to garnish
50g/2oz/¼ cup butter
salt and ground black pepper

1 Preheat the oven to 190°C/ 375°F/Gas 5. Put the clams into a large pan, cover with water and bring to the boil. Add a little salt then simmer until the shells open. Reserve the cooking liquor. Shell the clams, reserving a few whole.

2 Weigh the shelled clams. Then weigh the same amount of unpeeled potatoes. Peel and slice the potatoes thinly. Oil a flameproof dish. Arrange a layer of potatoes in the base of the dish, add a layer of clams and salt and pepper.

3 Repeat the layers until the ingredients are all used, finishing with a layer of potatoes on top.

4 Pour in some of the reserved cooking liquor to come about halfway up the dish. Dot the top with the butter, then cover with foil.

5 Bring to the boil on the stove over a medium-high heat, then bake in the preheated oven for 2 hours until the top is golden brown. Serve hot, garnished with chopped fresh flat leaf parsley.

Nutritional information per portion: Energy 320kcal/1348kJ; Protein 17.3g; Carbohydrate 36.7g, of which sugars 3.3g; Fat 12.6g, of which saturates 7g; Cholesterol 57mg; Calcium 188mg; Fibre 2.9g; Sodium 262mg.

Cockle pie

This seaside dish is sprinkled with grated cheese and browned under the grill, though it could equally well be topped with shortcrust or puff pastry and cooked in a hot oven.

SERVES 4 AS AN APPETIZER OR 2 AS A MAIN DISH

425ml/³/₄ pint/scant 2 cups milk
25g/1oz/2 tbsp butter, cut into small pieces
25g/1oz/¹/₄ cup plain (all-purpose) flour
150–200g/5¹/₂–7oz shelled cooked cockles (small clams)
100g/3¹/₂oz/1 cup mature cheese, such as Cheddar, grated
about 60ml/4 tbsp fresh breadcrumbs
salt and ground black pepper

1 To make the sauce, put the milk, butter, flour and seasoning into a pan. Over medium heat and stirring constantly with a whisk, bring to the boil and bubble gently for 2–3 minutes until thick, smooth and glossy.

2 Stir two-thirds of the cheese in to the sauce. Add the cockles and bring just to the boil.

3 Spoon the mixture into one large dish or four individual flameproof dishes. Then toss together the remaining cheese and the breadcrumbs.

4 Sprinkle the cheese and breadcrumb mixture over the cockle sauce. Put under a hot grill (broiler) until bubbling and golden, and serve straight away.

Nutritional information per portion: Energy 294kcal/1231kJ; Protein 16.8g; Carbohydrate 21.6g, of which sugars 5.6g; Fat 15.7g, of which saturates 9.9g; Cholesterol 64mg; Calcium 376mg; Fibre 0.5g; Sodium 562mg.

Casseroles and Curries

Unlike meat, fish doesn't generally lend

itself to long, slow cooking, but there

are still wonderfully flavourful and

sustaining casseroles and curries that

can be created. Often these recipes

come from Asian cuisines, where chillies

and spices are combined in creamy

sauces to enhance and showcase the

tender fish and shellfish.

Cod and bean stew with saffron and paprika

In this dish, everything is cooked in one pot – the chunks of fresh, flaky cod, made yellow with saffron, their flavour offset by the smoked, spiced beans.

SERVES 6–8

1 large red (bell) pepper
45ml/3 tbsp olive oil
4 rashers (strips) streaky (fatty) bacon, roughly chopped
4 garlic cloves, finely chopped
1 onion, sliced
10ml/2 tsp paprika
5ml/1 tsp smoked Spanish paprika
large pinch of saffron threads
400g/14oz can butter (lima) beans, drained and rinsed
about 600ml/1 pint/2½ cups fish stock
60ml/4 tbsp Thai fish sauce
6 plum tomatoes, quartered
350g/12oz skinned cod fillet, cut into large chunks
45ml/3 tbsp chopped fresh coriander (cilantro), plus a few sprigs, to garnish
salt and ground black pepper

1 Preheat the grill (broiler) and line the pan with foil. Halve the red pepper and scoop out the seeds.

2 Place, cut-side down, in the grill pan and grill (broil) under a hot heat for about 10–15 minutes, until the skin is charred. Put the pepper in a plastic bag, seal and leave for 10 minutes. Remove from the bag, peel off the skin and discard. Chop the pepper into large pieces.

3 Heat the olive oil in a pan and fry the bacon and garlic for 2 minutes, then add the onion. Cover the pan and cook for 5 minutes.

4 Stir in the paprika together with the saffron and its soaking water, and salt and pepper. Stir the beans into the pan and add enough stock to cover.

5 Simmer, uncovered, for about 15 minutes, stirring occasionally. Stir in the fish sauce, pepper and tomato. Add the cubes of cod and stir in the sauce. Cover and simmer for 5 minutes until cooked. Stir in the chopped coriander.

6 Serve the stew in warmed soup plates or bowls, garnished with the coriander sprigs.

Nutritional information per portion: Energy 186kcal/778kJ; Protein 14g; Carbohydrate 12g, of which sugars 5g; Fat 9g, of which saturates 2g; Cholesterol 29mg; Calcium 43mg; Fibre 4g; Sodium 355mg.

Haddock and beer casserole

The earthy flavour of wild mushrooms perfectly complements the delicate taste of the haddock steaks and creamy sauce in this satisfying dish. Beer makes a delicious addition to the sauce.

SERVES 4

150g/5oz/2 cups wild mushrooms
50g/2oz/¼ cup butter
2 large onions, roughly chopped
2 celery sticks, sliced
2 carrots, sliced
4 haddock steaks, about 85g/6½ oz each
300ml/½ pint/1¼ cups light lager
4 bay leaves
25g/1oz/¼ cup plain (all-purpose) flour
200ml/7fl oz/scant 1 cup double (heavy) cream
salt and ground black pepper, to taste
dill sprigs, to garnish

1 Preheat the oven to 190°C/375°F/Gas 5. Brush the mushrooms to remove any grit and only wash the caps briefly if necessary. Dry with kitchen paper and chop them.

2 Melt 25g/1oz/2 tbsp butter in a flameproof casserole, then add the onions, mushrooms, celery and carrots. Fry for about 8 minutes, or until golden brown.

3 Place the haddock steaks on top of the vegetables, then pour over the lager. Add the bay leaves and season well with salt and pepper.

4 Put the casserole in the preheated oven and cook for 20–25 minutes, or until the fish flakes easily when tested. Remove the fish and vegetables from the casserole with a slotted spoon and transfer to a serving dish. Cover and keep warm.

5 Melt the remaining butter in a pan, then add the flour and cook, stirring, for 2 minutes. Pour in the liquid from the casserole, mix well and simmer for 2–3 minutes. Add the cream and heat, without boiling. Serve the fish and vegetables with the sauce, garnished with dill sprigs.

Nutritional information per portion: Energy 564kcal/2346kJ; Protein 37g; Carbohydrate 17.9g, of which sugars 10.5g; Fat 38.8g, of which saturates 23.5g; Cholesterol 158mg; Calcium 106mg; Fibre 3.4g; Sodium 231mg.

Burbot stew

A large freshwater fish, burbot looks similar to monkfish and has soft but well-flavoured flesh. This hearty chowder can be served on its own as an appetizer or with bread for a main meal.

SERVES 4

1kg/2¼lb burbot or monkfish, with their bones, if filleted
20g/¾oz/1½ tbsp unsalted butter
1 onion, chopped
1 small celery stick, chopped
1 small leek, chopped
1 bay leaf
10 whole allspice
5 white peppercorns
1.5 litres/2½ pints/6¼ cups water
1 carrot, finely diced
500g/1¼lb potatoes, cubed
5ml/1 tsp plain white (all-purpose) flour
200ml/7fl oz/scant 1 cup double (heavy) cream
salt and ground white pepper
dill sprigs, to garnish

1 Fillet the fish or, if the fishmonger fillets it for you, ask him to reserve the bones and head. Cut the fish into large chunks.

2 Heat the butter in a pan, add the onion, celery, leek, fish bones, fish head and any fish trimmings. Fry for about 5 minutes until the vegetables are beginning to soften.

3 Add the bay leaf, allspice, peppercorns, salt and 1 litre/1¾ pints/4 cups of the water. Bring to the boil, then lower the heat and simmer very gently for 30 minutes.

4 Strain the stock through a sieve (strainer) into a clean pan. (You should be left with about 1 litre/1¾ pints/4 cups of liquid or add water to make up the correct amount.)

5 Add the carrot and potato to the stock and bring to the boil. Lower the heat and simmer until the potato is nearly cooked. Add the fish to the pan, return to a simmer, then sprinkle over the flour and simmer for a further 5 minutes, or until the fish is just cooked. Stir in the cream. Pour into serving dishes and serve garnished with a sprig of dill.

Nutritional information per portion: Energy 582kcal/2431kJ; Protein 47.6g; Carbohydrate 25.8g, of which sugars 6.4g; Fat 32.6g, of which saturates 19.7g; Cholesterol 119mg; Calcium 77mg; Fibre 2.8g; Sodium 117mg.

Fisherman's casserole

This simple recipe can be adapted to include whichever fish are available on the day. You can also use a dry white wine instead of the cider. Serve with crusty bread.

SERVES 4

500g/1¼lb mixed fish fillets, such as
   haddock, bass, red mullet or salmon
500g/1¼lb mixed shellfish, such as squid
   strips, mussels and prawns (shrimp)
15ml/1 tbsp oil
25g/1oz/2 tbsp butter
1 medium onion, finely chopped
1 carrot, finely chopped
3 celery sticks, finely chopped
30ml/2 tbsp plain (all-purpose) flour
600ml/1 pint/2½ cups fish stock
300ml/½ pt/1¼ cups dry (hard) cider
350g/12oz small new potatoes, halved
150m/¼ pint/²/₃ cup double (heavy)
   cream
a handful of chopped mixed herbs such as
   parsley, chives and dill
salt and ground black pepper

1 Wash the fish fillets and dry on kitchen paper. With a sharp knife, remove the skin, feel carefully for any bones, and extract them. Cut the fish into large, even chunks.

2 Scrub the mussels and cockles, discarding any with broken shells or that do not close when given a sharp tap. Pull off the beards.

3 Heat the oil and butter in a saucepan, add the onion, carrot and celery and cook, stirring, until beginning to soften. Add the flour, and cook, stirring, for 1 minute.

4 Remove the pan from the heat and gradually stir in the fish stock and cider. Return the pan to the heat and cook, stirring, until the mixture comes to the boil. Add the potatoes and bring back to the boil.

5 Cover the pan and simmer for 10–15 minutes until the potatoes are nearly tender. Add the fish and shellfish and stir in gently.

6 Stir in the cream. Gently simmer, then cover and cook for 5–10 minutes, until all the shells open. Season, add the herbs, and serve.

Nutritional information per portion: Energy 583kcal/2439kJ; Protein 49.3g; Carbohydrate 25.3g, of which sugars 6.1g; Fat 30.2g, of which saturates 16.5g; Cholesterol 354mg; Calcium 199mg; Fibre 2.5g; Sodium 404mg.

Grouper stewed with grapes

Fish stews are found in all Mediterranean cuisines and in other coastal regions of southern Europe. This one adds green grapes, which give an elegant acidity to the flavour.

SERVES 4

50ml/2fl oz/¼ cup olive oil

1 small onion, chopped

1 garlic clove, chopped

1 green (bell) pepper, seeded and chopped

1 bay leaf

1 ripe tomato, peeled and diced

5ml/1 tsp saffron threads

20 green grapes

200ml/7fl oz/scant 1 cup fish stock

4 grouper fillets with skin, each weighing about 175g/6oz

a small bunch of mint, chopped

1 Preheat the oven to 180°C/350°F/ Gas 4. Heat the oil in a flameproof casserole. Add the onion, garlic, green pepper and bay leaf, and cook over a low heat for 5 minutes, stirring occasionally, until the onion has softened.

2 Add the tomato and saffron to the casserole and cook, still stirring, for a few minutes more.

3 Add the grapes and stock to the casserole and bring to the boil.

4 Place the fish in the casserole, skin side up, cover and cook in the oven for about 20 minutes.

5 When the fish is cooked through and tender, stir through the mint. Serve in warmed bowls.

Nutritional information per portion: Energy 248kcal/1037kJ; Protein 33.2g; Carbohydrate 6.7g, of which sugars 6.1g; Fat 9.9g, of which saturates 1.4g; Cholesterol 81mg; Calcium 51mg; Fibre 1.9g; Sodium 114mg.

Sour fish, star fruit and chilli stew

Somewhere between a stew and a soup, this refreshing dish is just one of many variations on the theme of sour fish stew found throughout South-east Asia.

SERVES 4

30ml/2 tbsp coconut or palm oil
900ml/1½ pints/3¾ cups water
2 lemon grass stalks, bruised
25g/1oz fresh root ginger, finely sliced
about 675g/1½ lb trout, cut into steaks
2 firm star fruit (carambola), sliced
juice of 1–2 limes
steamed rice, to serve

FOR THE SPICE PASTE

4 shallots, chopped
4 red chillies, seeded and chopped
2 garlic cloves, chopped
25g/1oz galangal, chopped
25g/1oz fresh turmeric, chopped
3–4 candlenuts, chopped

1 Using a mortar and pestle, grind the spice paste ingredients to form a paste. Heat the oil in a wok or frying pan, stir in the spice paste and fry until fragrant. Pour in the water and add the lemon grass and ginger. Bring to the boil, then reduce the heat and simmer for 10 minutes.

2 Slip the fish steaks into the pan; add more water if necessary to just cover. Simmer for 3–4 minutes, then add the star fruit and lime juice. Simmer for a further 2–3 minutes.

3 Divide the fish and star fruit between warmed serving bowls and add a little of the cooking liquid. Serve with bowls of steamed rice, which is moistened by spoonfuls of the remaining cooking liquid.

Nutritional information per portion: Energy 240kcal/1001kJ; Protein 25.9g; Carbohydrate 7.3g, of which sugars 4.7g; Fat 12.1g, of which saturates 1.2g; Cholesterol 0mg; Calcium 27mg; Fibre 1.7g; Sodium 67mg.

Fragrant Spanish fish stew

This splendid fish feast, in which a variety of fish and shellfish are gently poached in a fragrant and tasty broth, is a great favourite throughout Spain. It is important not to overcook the seafood, so make sure you only leave it in the hot broth long enough to just cook through.

SERVES 6

60ml/4 tbsp olive oil
8 small squid, cleaned
plain (all-purpose) flour, for dusting
500g/1¼lb skinless, boneless white fish
   such as monkfish and cod, cut in
   large chunks
30ml/2 tbsp Ricard or Pernod
450ml/¾ pint/2 cups fish stock
250ml/8fl oz/1 cup white wine
450g/1lb mussels, cleaned
16 raw king prawns (jumbo shrimp),
   with heads, shelled and deveined

115g/4oz prawns (shrimp)
salt and ground black pepper
45ml/3 tbsp chopped fresh parsley, to garnish

FOR THE BROTH
30ml/2 tbsp oil
1 large onion, finely chopped
2 garlic cloves, finely chopped
500g/1¼lb ripe tomatoes, peeled, seeded and chopped
2 bay leaves
1 dried chilli, seeded and chopped
5ml/1 tsp paprika
a pinch of saffron threads

1 To make the broth, heat the oil in a flameproof casserole and soften the onion and garlic. Add the tomatoes, bay leaves, chilli, paprika and saffron and cook gently to make a sauce.

2 Meanwhile, heat the oil in a large pan. Put in the squid tentacles, face down, and cook for 45 seconds, to make 'flowers'. Reserve on a plate. Flour and fry the fish pieces for 2 minutes on each side. Cut the squid bodies into rings and fry. Pour the Ricard or Pernod into a ladle, flame it and pour over the fish remaining in the pan. Remove the fish and reserve.

3 Add the fish stock and the wine to the sauce and bring to a simmer. Add the mussels, cover for 2 minutes, then remove to a plate, discard any closed mussels, and remove the upper shells. Add the raw prawns to the casserole for 3–4 minutes, then lift out and reserve.

4 Add the white fish to the casserole, simmer gently for 5 minutes, then add the squid rings and the prawns, keeping a gentle simmer. After another 2–3 minutes add the mussels, simmer for another minute, season to taste. Sprinkle over the squid flowers, garnish with parsley and serve.

Nutritional information per portion: Energy 463kcal/1940kJ; Protein 30g; Carbohydrate 32.3g, of which sugars 13.8g; Fat 21.7g, of which saturates 6.5g; Cholesterol 61mg; Calcium 80mg; Fibre 4.2g; Sodium 738mg.

Fish goulash

A remnant of the Austro-Hungarian Empire, goulash remains a classic Hungarian dish, and is often made with fish rather than meat. It is flavoured with paprika and served with sour cream.

SERVES 4

1.2kg/2½ lb mixed fish

2 bay leaves

30ml/2 tbsp olive oil

1 large onion, chopped

2 celery sticks, chopped

1 green (bell) pepper, seeded and
  chopped

2 garlic cloves, chopped

75g/3oz lean smoked back bacon rashers
  (strips), rinded and diced

15ml/1 tbsp plain (all-purpose) flour

15ml/1 tbsp paprika

5ml/1 tsp chopped fresh thyme

200g/7oz can chopped tomatoes

75g/3oz fine green beans, cut into
  bitesize lengths

30ml/2 tbsp chopped fresh parsley

salt and ground black pepper

sour cream, to serve

1 Skin and fillet the fish and cut the flesh into chunks. Put the fish heads and bones into a large pan together with the bay leaves. Barely cover with cold water and bring to the boil. Gently simmer for 30 minutes. Skim and strain the stock.

2 Heat the oil in a large pan, add the onion and gently cook for 5 minutes, until the onion is softened and translucent. Stir in the celery, green pepper, garlic and bacon, and cook for a further 3–4 minutes. Stir in the flour and paprika and cook for 1 more minute.

3 Gradually add 600ml/1 pint/2½ cups of the fish stock. Add the thyme, chopped tomatoes and salt and pepper. Cover and simmer for 5 minutes or until the vegetables are almost tender.

4 Add the green beans, fish chunks and parsley and cook for about 10 minutes or until the fish and all the vegetables are cooked.

5 Ladle into warmed deep plates or bowls, and serve with a generous spoonful of sour cream and a sprinkle of paprika.

Nutritional information per portion: Energy 382kcal/1603kJ; Protein 60.2g; Carbohydrate 9.4g, of which sugars 4.9g; Fat 11.7g, of which saturates 2.4g; Cholesterol 148mg; Calcium 60mg; Fibre 1.9g; Sodium 486mg.

Malay fish curry

The fish curries of Malaysia differ slightly from region to region, but most of them include Indian spices and coconut milk. They are usually served with bread or rice, pickles and extra chillies.

SERVES 4

4 shallots, chopped
4 garlic cloves, chopped
50g/2oz fresh root ginger, peeled and
 chopped
25g/1oz fresh turmeric, chopped
4–6 dried red chillies, softened in warm
 water and chopped
15ml/1 tbsp coriander seeds, roasted
15ml/1 tbsp cumin seeds, roasted
10ml/2 tsp fish curry powder
5ml/1 tsp fennel seeds
2.5ml/½ tsp black peppercorns
30ml/2 tbsp vegetable oil
7.5ml/1½ tsp tamarind paste
8 thick fish cutlets, about 90g/3½ oz,
 such as grouper, red snapper or trout
800ml/1½ pints coconut milk
salt

1 First make the curry paste. In a food processor, grind the shallots, garlic, ginger, turmeric and chillies to a paste and transfer to a bowl.

2 Again, use the food processor to grind the roasted coriander and cumin seeds, fish curry powder, fennel seeds and peppercorns to a powder and add to the paste in the bowl. Mix with 15ml/1 tbsp water.

3 Heat the oil in a wok or heavy pan. Stir in the curry paste and fry until fragrant.

4 Add the tamarind paste and mix well. Add the fish cutlets and cook for 1 minute on each side. Pour in the coconut milk, mix well and bring to the boil.

5 Reduce the heat and simmer for 10–15 minutes until the fish is cooked. Season to taste with salt.

6 Scatter the coriander over the top and serve with plain or yellow rice, or with chunks of crusty bread to mop up the sauce.

Nutritional information per portion: Energy 304kcal/1281kJ; Protein 38g; Carbohydrate 16g, of which sugars 13g; Fat 12g, of which saturates 2g; Cholesterol 67mg; Calcium 193mg; Fibre 0g; Sodium 373mg.

Fish with spinach and lime

Fresh herbs and hot spices are combined to make the charmoula marinade that is used to flavour this delicious Moroccan-style dish.

SERVES 4

675g/1½ lb white fish, such as haddock, cod or sea bass, cleaned and skinned
sunflower oil, for frying
500g/1¼lb potatoes, sliced
1 onion, chopped
1–2 garlic cloves, crushed
5 tomatoes, peeled and chopped
375g/13oz fresh spinach, chopped
lime wedges, to garnish

FOR THE CHARMOULA

6 spring onions (scallions), chopped
10ml/2 tsp fresh thyme
60ml/4 tbsp chopped parsley
30ml/2 tbsp chopped coriander (cilantro)
10ml/2 tsp paprika
a generous pinch of cayenne pepper
60ml/4 tbsp olive oil
grated rind and juice of 1 lime
salt

1 Cut the fish into even-size pieces and place in a large shallow dish. Blend the ingredients for the charmoula, add salt and pour over the fish. Leave in a cool place, covered, to marinate for 2–4 hours.

2 Heat 5mm/¼ in oil in a heavy pan, add the potato slices and cook, turning, until they are cooked through. Remove from the pan.

3 Pour off most of the oil and add the onion, garlic and tomatoes. Cook over a gentle heat for 5–6 minutes until soft. Place the potatoes on top, then add the spinach.

4 Place the marinated fish pieces on the spinach in the pan and pour over all of the marinade. Cover the pan and cook for 15–18 minutes.

5 After 8 minutes of the cooking time, stir the contents of the pan, so that the fish at the top are distributed throughout the dish.

6 Cover the pan and continue cooking, but be careful not to overcook – it is ready once the fish is just tender and opaque and the spinach has wilted. Serve hot, with wedges of lime and warm crusty bread, if you like.

Nutritional information per portion: Energy 433Kcal/1810kJ; Protein 37.3g; Carbohydrate 28.9g, of which sugars 9.4g; Fat 19.3g, of which saturates 2.8g; Cholesterol 78mg; Calcium 206mg; Fibre 5.2g; Sodium 260mg.

Goan fish casserole

The cooking of the Indian region of Goa is a mixture of Portuguese and Indian; the addition of tamarind gives a tangy note to the spicy coconut sauce.

SERVES 4

7.5ml/1½ tsp ground turmeric

5ml/1 tsp salt

450g/1lb monkfish fillet, cut into eight

15ml/1 tbsp lemon juice

5ml/1 tsp cumin seeds

5ml/1 tsp coriander seeds

5ml/1 tsp black peppercorns

1 garlic clove, chopped

5cm/2in piece fresh root ginger, grated

25g/1oz tamarind paste

150ml/¼ pint/⅔ cup hot water

30ml/2 tbsp vegetable oil

2 onions, halved and sliced lengthways

400ml/14fl oz/1⅔ cups coconut milk

4 green chillies, seeded and cut into strips

16 large raw prawns (shrimp), peeled

30ml/2 tbsp chopped fresh coriander
   (cilantro) leaves, to garnish

1 Mix the turmeric and salt in a small bowl. Place the monkfish in a dish and sprinkle with the lemon juice, then rub the turmeric mixture over the fish fillets to coat.

2 Put the cumin seeds, coriander seeds and peppercorns in a small food processor and blend to a powder. Add the garlic and ginger and process for a few seconds more. Preheat the oven to 200°C/400°F/Gas 6. Mix the tamarind paste with the hot water. Set aside.

3 Heat the oil in a frying pan, add the onions and cook until soft.

4 Transfer the onions to an ovenproof dish. Add the fish to the pan, and fry on a high heat, turning to seal all sides. Remove the fish from the pan and place on top of the onions. Add the spice mixture to the pan and cook for 1–2 minutes.

5 Add the tamarind liquid, coconut milk and chillies and bring to the boil. Pour the sauce over the fish. Cover, and bake for 10 minutes.

6 Add the prawns, cover again and return it to the oven for 5 minutes. Check the seasoning, sprinkle with coriander leaves and serve.

Nutritional information per portion: Energy 220Kcal/926kJ; Protein 28g; Carbohydrate 12.8g, of which sugars 10.5g; Fat 6.8g, of which saturates 1g; Cholesterol 113mg; Calcium 103mg; Fibre 1.4g; Sodium 720mg.

Fish in an aromatic sauce

This well-loved dish from West Bengal is flavoured with mustard oil and a combination of five whole spices that produces a memorable aromatic taste.

SERVES 4–5

675g/1½ lb fillets of tilapia or other firm white
    fish, cut into 5cm/2in pieces
5ml/1 tsp ground turmeric
5ml/1 tsp salt or to taste
4 tbsp vegetable oil
1.5ml/¼ tsp black mustard seeds
1.5ml/¼ tsp cumin seeds
1.5ml/¼ tsp fennel seeds
1.5ml/¼ tsp nigella seeds
5–6 fenugreek seeds
2 bay leaves

2 dried red chillies, left whole
2 fresh green chillies, chopped
2.5ml/½ tsp ground cumin
5ml/1 tsp ground coriander
75g/3oz chopped canned tomatoes
115g/4oz potatoes, cubed
115g/4oz aubergine (eggplant), cubed
50g/2oz/½ cup frozen peas
30ml/2 tbsp chopped fresh coriander (cilantro)
plain boiled rice, to serve

1 Lay the fish on a large plate and rub in half the turmeric and half the salt. Set aside. Heat half the oil over a medium heat, then remove from the heat and add the mustard seeds, cumin, fennel, nigella and fenugreek seeds.

2 Add the bay leaves, and the red and green chillies. Return the pan to the heat and add the ground cumin and coriander and remaining turmeric. Stir, then add the tomatoes. Cook for 4–5 minutes.

3 Add in all the potato cubes and the aubergine pieces, along with about 350ml/12fl oz/1½ cups warm water and the remaining salt. Bring the pan to the boil, then reduce the heat to low, cover and cook for 15 minutes, stirring occasionally.

4 Meanwhile, heat the remaining oil in a frying pan until almost smoking. Fry the fish in batches until well browned and drain on absorbent paper. Add the fried fish to the curry along with the peas. Cook for 4–5 minutes, then stir in the chopped coriander and remove from the heat. Serve with plain rice.

Nutritional information per portion: Energy 242kcal/1011kJ; Protein 27.1g; Carbohydrate 7.4g, of which sugars 1.4g; Fat 11.9g, of which saturates 1.5g; Cholesterol 0mg; Calcium 184mg; Fibre 1.2g; Sodium 83mg.

Dry fish stew with coriander

A seco is a 'dry' style of stew that can be made with fish or meat. The recipe, from the northern region of Peru, uses coriander and other locally grown ingredients. The cooking of the north includes many versions of seco made with chicken, kid, goat and lamb.

SERVES 6

6 swordfish steaks

1 large red onion, sliced lengthways

1 red (bell) pepper, thinly sliced

3 garlic cloves

2.5cm/1in piece fresh root ginger

100g/3¾oz chopped fresh coriander (cilantro)

1.5ml/¼ tsp ground cumin

45ml/3 tbsp chilli sauce

120ml/4fl oz/½ cup vegetable oil

120ml/4fl oz/½ cup white beer

250g/9oz/2 cups shelled peas

juice of 1 lime

salt and ground black pepper

boiled rice, to serve

1 Arrange the swordfish steaks in a wide pan and cover with the slices of onion and red pepper.

2 Put the garlic cloves, fresh root ginger, coriander, cumin, chilli sauce and oil into a blender or food processor, and blend to a purée.

3 Spoon the mixture over the fish and leave to marinate in the saucepan for about 15 minutes.

4 Put the pan on a high heat until the fish is starting to sizzle, pour in the beer and add the peas, and bring to the boil. Reduce the heat, cover the pan and simmer for 15 minutes. When the fish is cooked, squeeze the lime juice over the top, and serve with rice.

COOK'S TIP

Since swordfish is inclined to be rather dry, any recipe that marinates the fish in a mixture of spices and oil is ideal. Although it is technically a white fish, swordfish has a firm, meaty texture.

Nutritional information per portion: Energy 302kcal/1257kJ; Protein 31.5g; Carbohydrate 9.6g, of which sugars 5.4g; Fat 14.9g, of which saturates 1.6g; Cholesterol 69mg; Calcium 63mg; Fibre 3.5g; Sodium 183mg.

Cuttlefish with potatoes

Similar to squid, cuttlefish is sweeter and more tender, provided you buy small or medium-sized specimens. If the only ones available are very large, cook them for a little longer.

SERVES 4

1kg/2¼lb fresh cuttlefish
150ml/¼ pint/⅔ cup virgin olive oil
1 large onion, about 225g/8oz, chopped
1 glass white wine, about 175ml/6fl
    oz/¾ cup
300ml/½ pint/1¼ cups hot water
500g/1¼lb potatoes, peeled and cubed
4–5 spring onions (scallions), chopped
juice of 1 lemon
60ml/4 tbsp chopped fresh dill
salt and ground black pepper

1 Prepare the cuttlefish, following the instructions for preparing squid on page 44. Rinse and drain, then slice into 2cm/¾in wide ribbons.

2 Heat the oil in a heavy pan, add the onion and sauté for about 5 minutes until light golden. Add the cuttlefish and sauté until all the water they exude has evaporated and the flesh starts to change colour. This will take 10–15 minutes.

3 Pour in the wine and, when it has evaporated, add the water. Cover and cook for 10 minutes, then add the potatoes, spring onions, lemon juice, and salt and pepper.

4 Add enough water to almost cover the ingredients; top up if necessary. Cover and cook gently for 40 minutes or until the cuttlefish is tender, stirring occasionally. Stir in the dill and serve hot.

Nutritional information per portion: Energy 423kcal/1761kJ; Protein 29g; Carbohydrate 18g, of which sugars 3g; Fat 26g, of which saturates 4g; Cholesterol 183mg; Calcium 123mg; Fibre 2g; Sodium 625mg.

Mediterranean squid with olives and red wine

This is one of the most memorable squid dishes from around the Mediterranean coast. Chunks of crusty bread and a leafy green salad make good accompaniments.

SERVES 4

30–45ml/2–3 tbsp olive oil
2 red onions, chopped
3–4 garlic cloves, chopped
750g/1lb 10oz squid, cleaned
45–60ml/3–4 tbsp black olives, pitted
5–10ml/1–2 tsp ground cinnamon
5–10ml/1–2 tsp sugar
about 300ml/½ pint/1¼ cups red wine
2 bay leaves
1 small bunch each of fresh flat leaf
    parsley and dill, finely chopped
salt and ground black pepper
lemon wedges, to serve

1 Cut the squid into thick rings. Heat the oil in a heavy pan and cook the onions and garlic until golden. Add the squid rings and toss them in the pan for 2–3 minutes, until they begin to colour.

2 Toss in the olives, cinnamon and sugar, pour in the wine and add the bay leaves. Boil, then lower the heat and cover the pan.

3 Cook for 35–40 minutes, until most of the liquid has reduced and the squid is tender. Season and add the herbs. Serve with lemon wedges.

COOK'S TIP
To prepare the squid, peel off the skin, then sever the head and trim the tentacles with a sharp knife. Pull out the 'quill' and remove the ink sac and any mushy bits. Rinse inside and out.

Nutritional information per portion: Energy 304kcal/1275kJ; Protein 30.3g; Carbohydrate 11.4g, of which sugars 6.8g; Fat 10.1g, of which saturates 1.7g; Cholesterol 422mg; Calcium 62mg; Fibre 1.7g; Sodium 468mg.

Eel braised in caramel sauce

This is a Vietnamese dish, with different versions depending on the region. It is traditionally a northern dish, however, and it is there, in the highlands, that it is best sampled, where the eels are caught in the Red, Black and Song Ma rivers. If you cannot obtain eel, use mackerel. When it is cooked in this way, the eel is usually served with noodles or rice.

SERVES 4

45ml/3 tbsp raw cane sugar

30ml/2 tbsp soy sauce

45ml/3 tbsp Thai fish sauce

2 garlic cloves, crushed

2 dried chillies

2–3 star anise

4–5 peppercorns

350g/12oz eel on the bone, cut into 2.5cm/1in-thick chunks

200g/7oz butternut squash, cut into bitesize chunks

4 spring onions (scallions), cut into bitesize pieces

30ml/2 tbsp sesame oil

5cm/2in fresh root ginger, peeled and cut into matchsticks

salt

boiled rice, to serve

1 Put the sugar in a heavy pan or wok with 30ml/2 tbsp water, and gently heat it until it turns golden. Remove the pan from the heat and stir in the soy sauce and fish sauce with 120ml/4fl oz/½ cup water. Add the garlic, chillies, star anise and peppercorns, and return to the heat.

2 Add the eel chunks to the pan with the squash and spring onions, making sure the fish is well coated in the sauce. Season with salt. Reduce the heat, cover the pan and simmer for about 20 minutes to let the eel braise gently in the sauce and steam.

3 Meanwhile, heat a small wok, add the oil and stir-fry the ginger until crisp and golden. Remove and drain on kitchen paper.

4 When the eel is nicely tender, arrange it on a warmed serving dish, scatter the crispy ginger over it, and serve with boiled rice.

Nutritional information per portion: Energy 204Kcal/857kJ; Protein 11g; Carbohydrate 20g, of which sugars 14g; Fat 10g, of which saturates 1g; Cholesterol 0mg; Calcium 76mg; Fibre 1g; Sodium 1.1g.

King prawns in a coconut cream

Coconut milk is used to make a luxurious sauce thickened with cashews, peanuts and breadcrumbs in this wonderfully full-flavoured prawn dish.

SERVES 6

130g/4½oz/2¼ cups fresh white
 breadcrumbs
105ml/7 tbsp coconut milk
900g/2lb raw king prawns (jumbo
 shrimp), peeled, shells reserved
400ml/14fl oz/1⅔ cups fish stock
2 large tomatoes, chopped
1 onion, quartered
2 fresh red chillies, seeded and chopped
130g/4½oz dried shrimps
45ml/3 tbsp palm oil
2 garlic cloves, crushed
25g/1oz fresh root ginger, grated
75g/3oz/¾ cup roasted peanuts and
 50g/2oz/½ cup cashew nuts, ground
 to a fine powder
60ml/4 tbsp coconut cream
juice of 1 lime
salt and ground black pepper
steamed white rice and hot chilli oil,
 to serve

1 Place the breadcrumbs in a bowl and stir in the coconut milk. Leave to soak for at least 30 minutes. Purée, in a food processor, then scrape into a bowl and set aside.

2 Place the prawn shells in a pan with the fish stock and tomatoes. Bring to the boil, then simmer for 30 minutes. Strain into a bowl, pressing the shells against the sides of the sieve to extract as much flavour as possible. Reserve the prawn stock but discard the shells.

3 Blend the onion, chillies and dried shrimps to a purée. Scrape into a pan and add the oil.

4 Cook gently for 5 minutes. Add the garlic and ginger and cook for 2 minutes more. Add the powdered nuts to the pan and cook for a further 1 minute. Stir in the breadcrumb purée and prawn stock and bring to the boil.

5 Reduce the heat and continue to cook, stirring, for 6–8 minutes, until thick and smooth. Add the coconut cream, lime juice and prawns. Stir over the heat for 3 minutes.

6 When the prawns are cooked, season and serve with steamed rice, adding a couple of drops of chilli oil to each portion.

Nutritional information per portion: Energy 368kcal/1538kJ; Protein 23g; Carbohydrate 19g, of which sugars 6g; Fat 23g, of which saturates 9g; Cholesterol 139mg; Calcium 321mg; Fibre 3g; Sodium 1296mg.

Aromatic prawn laksa

This is a hearty dish, and is perfect when you are tired. Tiger prawns, vegetables and noodles are tangled together in a savoury coconut broth – flavours and textures that soothe and stimulate.

SERVES 4

6 dried red chillies

1 onion, chopped

5cm/2in fresh root ginger, grated

5ml/1 tsp ground turmeric

45ml/3 tbsp Thai fish sauce

finely grated rind of 1 lime

8 macadamia nuts

5ml/1 tsp ground coriander

60ml/4 tbsp vegetable oil

475ml/16fl oz/2 cups fish stock

750ml/1¼ pints/3 cups coconut milk

225g/8oz dried flat rice noodles

120ml/4fl oz/½ cup coconut cream

400g/14oz raw headless tiger prawns
   (jumbo shrimp), shelled and deveined,
   with tails left

225g/8oz/4 cups fresh beansprouts

coriander (cilantro) sprigs, to serve

1 Soak the chillies in warm water for 30 minutes. Drain them, cut them in half and remove the seeds. Put the chillies, onion, ginger, turmeric, fish sauce, lime rind, macadamia nuts, ground coriander and half of the vegetable oil into a food processor or blender and process to form a smooth paste.

2 Heat the remaining oil in a pan, add the paste and fry for 5 minutes, stirring all the time to prevent sticking. Add the fish stock and simmer for a further 5 minutes.

3 Pour in the canned coconut milk, stirring to prevent curdling. Bring to the boil and simmer, uncovered, for about 5 minutes. Meanwhile, cook the noodles in a separate pan of boiling water according to the packet instructions, drain and toss in a little oil. Set aside.

4 Stir the thick coconut milk and prawns into the soup. Simmer for a further 2–3 minutes. To serve, add noodles to serving bowls. Add the beansprouts and prawns, pour over the soup, add coriander and serve.

Nutritional information per portion: Energy 544kcal/2276kJ; Protein 29g; Carbohydrate 63g, of which sugars 13g; Fat 19g, of which saturates 3g; Cholesterol 244mg; Calcium 192mg; Fibre 4g; Sodium 1143mg.

Spicy prawn casserole

This popular Turkish prawn dish is often served as part of a hot meze in the fish restaurants of Izmir and Istanbul, but it is also good served as a main meal with a green salad and flatbread.

SERVES 4

30–45ml/2–3 tbsp olive oil
1 onion, finely sliced
1 green (bell) pepper, seeded and sliced
2–3 garlic cloves, chopped
5–10ml/1–2 tsp coriander seeds
1 fresh red chilli, seeded and chopped
5–10ml/1–2 tsp sugar
a splash of white wine vinegar
2 x 400g/14oz cans chopped tomatoes
1 bunch of fresh parsley, chopped
500g/1¼lb fresh raw prawns (shrimp)
120g/4oz Parmesan cheese, grated
salt and ground black pepper

1 Heat the oil in a heavy pan, stir in the onion, green pepper, garlic, coriander seeds and chopped chilli and cook until softened. Stir in the sugar, vinegar, tomatoes and parsley, then cook gently for about 25 minutes, until thickened.

2 While the sauce is cooking, shell the prawns. Peheat the oven to 200°C/400°F/Gas 6.

3 Season the sauce with salt and pepper and add the prawns. Heat through for 1 minute and then test for seasoning.

4 Spoon the mixture into individual earthenware pots and sprinkle the top with the grated cheese. Bake in the oven for 15 minutes, or until the cheese is melted and nicely browned on top.

Nutritional information per portion: Energy 338kcal/1413kJ; Protein 35.9g; Carbohydrate 11.2g, of which sugars 10.8g; Fat 16.9g, of which saturates 7.3g; Cholesterol 274mg; Calcium 481mg; Fibre 2.9g; Sodium 585mg.

Octopus stew

In the north of Spain, octopus stews are very popular, and are a favourite tapas dish, served on little wooden plates. Here octopus is stewed with tomatoes and potatoes, to make a main course.

SERVES 4–6

1kg/2¼lb octopus, cleaned
45ml/3 tbsp olive oil
1 large red onion, chopped
3 garlic cloves, finely chopped
30ml/2 tbsp brandy
300ml/½ pint/1¼ cups dry white wine
2 x 400g/14oz cans chopped tomatoes
1 dried red chilli, seeded and chopped
1.5ml/¼ tsp paprika
450g/1lb small new potatoes
15ml/1 tbsp chopped fresh rosemary
15ml/1 tbsp fresh thyme leaves
1.2 litres/2 pints/5 cups fish stock
30ml/2 tbsp chopped fresh flat leaf
    parsley leaves
salt and ground black pepper
rosemary sprigs, to garnish
salad leaves and French bread, to serve

1 Cut the octopus into large pieces, put in a pan and pour in cold water to cover. Season with salt, bring to the boil, then lower the heat and simmer for 30 minutes to tenderize it. Drain and cut into bitesize pieces.

2 Heat the oil in a large shallow pan. Fry the onion until lightly coloured, then add the garlic and fry for 1 minute. Add the octopus and fry for 2–3 minutes, stirring, until coloured.

3 Pour the brandy over the octopus and ignite it.

4 When the flames have died down, add the wine. Bring to the boil and bubble gently for about 5 minutes. Stir in the chopped tomatoes, with the chilli and paprika, then add the potatoes, rosemary and thyme. Simmer gently for 5 minutes.

5 Pour in the fish stock. Cover and simmer for 20–30 minutes, stirring occasionally, until the octopus and potatoes are tender and the sauce has thickened slightly. To serve, check the seasoning and stir in the parsley. Garnish with rosemary and accompany with salad and bread.

Nutritional information per portion: Energy 325kcal/1369kJ; Protein 32.7g; Carbohydrate 20.5g, of which sugars 8.2g; Fat 8.4g, of which saturates 1.5g; Cholesterol 80mg; Calcium 86mg; Fibre 2.8g; Sodium 24mg.

Yellow prawn curry

This south-east Asian speciality lives up to its name, with an intense yellow colour from the turmeric that matches the strong flavours.

SERVES 4

30ml/2 tbsp coconut or palm oil

2 shallots, finely chopped

2 garlic cloves, finely chopped

2 red chillies, seeded and finely chopped

10ml/2 tsp ground turmeric

25g/1oz fresh root ginger, finely chopped

2 lemon grass stalks, finely sliced

10ml/2 tsp coriander seeds

10ml/2 tsp shrimp paste

1 red (bell) pepper, seeded and sliced

4 kaffir lime leaves

about 500g/1¼lb fresh prawns (shrimp), shelled and deveined

400g/14oz can coconut milk

salt and ground black pepper

1 green chilli, seeded and sliced, and cooked white rice, to serve

1 Heat the oil in a wok or heavy frying pan. Stir in the shallots, garlic, chillies, turmeric, ginger, lemon grass and coriander seeds and fry until the fragrant aromas are released.

2 Stir the shrimp paste in to the pan and cook for 2–3 minutes. Add the red pepper and lime leaves and stir-fry for a further 1 minute.

3 Add the prawns to the pan. Pour in the coconut milk and bring to the boil, stirring. Cook for 5–6 minutes.

4 When the prawns are cooked, season with salt and pepper to taste. Spoon the prawns on to a warmed serving dish.

5 Sprinkle with the sliced green chilli and serve with rice.

VARIATION

Big, juicy prawns are delectable in this dish, but you can easily substitute them for small prawns or crayfish tails, depending on what is available.

Nutritional information per portion: Energy 230kcal/965kJ; Protein 26.4g; Carbohydrate 16g, of which sugars 13.5g; Fat 7.2g, of which saturates 1g; Cholesterol 263mg; Calcium 226mg; Fibre 2.7g; Sodium 519mg.

Whelks and potatoes in red chilli sauce

The South Pacific produces a wealth of shellfish, and local cooks have devised many recipes. One of these is the picante, which is a spicy stew of whelks and potatoes.

SERVES 4

75ml/5 tbsp vegetable oil

1 large red onion, finely chopped

15ml/1 tbsp chilli sauce

500g/1¼lb white potatoes, peeled and
    cut into 2cm/¾in cubes

2 fish or vegetable stock (bouillon) cubes
    dissolved in 500ml/17fl oz/generous
    2 cups water

500g/1¼lb cooked whelks, halved

salt

15ml/1 tbsp chopped parsley, to garnish

boiled rice, to serve

1 Heat the oil and fry the onion over high heat for 3 minutes, then reduce the heat to medium and cook for a further 7 minutes, until starting to brown. Stir in the chilli sauce. Add the potatoes and the stock to the pan, bring to the boil and cook for 20 minutes.

2 Add the whelks to the pan, and simmer for a further 5 minutes

3 When the whelks are heated through, check the seasoning then transfer to a serving dish, sprinkle with the chopped parsley and serve with boiled rice.

Nutritional information per portion: Energy 362kcal/1514kJ; Protein 27.9g; Carbohydrate 28.2g, of which sugars 7.3g; Fat 16g, of which saturates 1.8g; Cholesterol 156mg; Calcium 138mg; Fibre 2.7g; Sodium 577mg.

Index